RACHZ

The True Story of a Fox

Rachz aged 10 months.

RACHZ

The True Story of a Fox

by

SUE CHAMBERS

ORIEL PRESS

STOCKSFIELD

BOSTON . MELBOURNE . HENLEY . LONDON

To
My dear husband Tom,
with love.
Without him this book
would not have been
possible, and to
My mother.

CONTENTS

CHAPTER ONE — *THE SURVIVOR*

T HE VIXEN lifted her head. She stepped warily and with a more than usual alertness as she breathed in the cold evening air. Most of the scents drawn in at the same time were familiar. She recognised the old scent of a rabbit she had relished a few days ago, coupled with those of a rotting tree-trunk and the fir trees growing in the copse where she lived.

There was another scent, too. One that she had come across two years previously. It made her stop in her tracks. She scented the air again, lifting her head higher as she did so. What was this unknown scent that told her instinctively it was to be feared? She stood for a few moments longer, but knew that if she was to be in time she must reach the den she had selected a couple of weeks ago.

During one particular fearsome storm that Autumn a large tree had fallen, taking with it two or three others that were in its way as it cracked and crashed to the leaf-covered ground below. As branches fell, and broke, and slid, and intermingled one with another, they formed a natural shelter, and it was just this that the vixen had come across.

She had had to forsake her usual method of digging out a large rabbit burrow or badger's earth, as this particular winter had been hard and cold, with deep snow covering the ground well into March. Not only that, the icy winds that penetrated the copse had encouraged the earth for miles around to freeze into an unyielding surface so that even her sharp claws could not make any worthwhile impression on it.

The ground beneath the fallen trees had remained dry and no snow had blown — Nature had come to her aid as if it knew, and provided her with a natural and weather-proof den.

The vixen continued her stealthy walk and stopped outside the entrance to the den, looking about her, still wary of that unknown scent lingering in the now still but freezing air. She backed into the tunnel of leaves and branches, not daring to turn round until she was a good four to five feet inside. Now, feeling safe enough to turn, she scuttled the last few feet until she came to the centre of the fallen pile of trees. Here she stood, yet again, hardly breathing, ears pricked forward, listening. Confident, at last, that she was going to be safe she lay down, but did not sleep.

The following morning was still and quiet. The sky was clear, but the air was bitterly cold. A shaft of weak wintry sunshine struck the mass of tangled trees and branches. The warm rays would do nothing to help them back to life, but despite this, life there was, for during the comforting closeness of the night the vixen had quietly given birth to four cubs.

She did not leave the den for two whole days. She did not need to for Nature had provided for her in the form of the afterbirth, or placenta, through which each cub was nourished whilst inside the vixen. When the cubs no longer needed them they provided nourishment for the mother, thus not only ensuring a good supply of milk due to their hormone content, but also helping her strength by supplying her with iron and vitamins.

She finally left the den for the first time at dusk on the

second day, but was not away for very long. Just long enough to relieve herself. Even such a simple action had to be carried out with all due care, though, and this she did by taking a complicated route, crossing her own trail a couple of times before selecting a spot some two hundred yards away from the den.

The return journey was no less complicated and every so often she would stand, absolutely still, listening and scenting for any danger, before finally wending her way back to her cubs. They had been born, as are all fox cubs, with their eyes still shut and their ears closed, but by the time they were about twelve days old their eyes would be open and their ears would follow about two days later. Their fur, even at this age, was close and dense, nature's protection against the cold.

They would only scramble about at feeding time, after which they would snuggle up against each other to conserve their body heat, so it was quite safe for them to be left for a few minutes at this stage in their lives.

For the next week this was their routine, feeding and sleeping, while the vixen ventured forth only three times to relieve herself and catch an unwary rabbit or sparrow.

THE NINTH DAY

The cubs were now nine days old and had changed from their initial rather shapeless appearance. They were getting fat round tummies and their legs had lengthened. Their eyes were beginning to 'crack' at the inner corner allowing only a modest amount of light in since they were still in their nest in the den. Each day from now on their eyes would open more and more, until by about the twelfth day they would be totally open, though at this stage not actually focusing properly. Contrary to what some people may think young animals' eyes do not open all of a sudden. It is a gradual process designed to occur before they can actually walk, or perhaps a better word would be stumble, about a little at approximately three weeks old.

Their demand for food was increasing due to their rapid growth rate and the vixen had just about used up her reserves and was looking a great deal thinner. It was time to get out and do some *real* hunting, for if she did not get a good meal on a fairly regular basis from now on then her body would be unable to produce the milk for the cubs and they were not yet at the stage where they could eat her regurgitated offerings. So, on the ninth day she fed the cubs, washed them, nuzzled them into a warm heap, looked at them, licked them and then made her way to the den entrance. It was blocked. A heavy snowfall during the night had covered everything and in places it was two to three feet deep. Anyway, this slight problem was skilfully solved by the vixen as she dug her way out, using her sharp nose and the strong claws on her forefeet.

It is unusual for foxes to hunt during the daylight hours, but hunger causes many nocturnal animals to flout the usual laws of nature, yet even doing this, nature was still on their side. At night-time the temperature would drop very, very low and any animal out hunting then would be using far more energy simply to retain its bodyheat. So if they hunted by day, the temperature would be higher and they would conserve their energy a little. Nature seems to think of everything!

By now the vixen was standing outside the den entrance. It had only been a small task, but her efforts had left her breathless and as she stood allowing time to settle her breathing a little, it was plain to see she was thin, as her flanks had sunk and her rib-cage showed with each deep breath, despite her thick, dense coat.

The winter sunshine seemed to have given the birds a new lease of life, for they sang and twittered among the snow-encrusted branches and flew from tree to tree looking in vain for an insect or berry that would help sustain them through another cold night. It looked very much as though there would be some casualties among the birds that day. But those birds would then be extra food for the vixen should she chance upon one, for what little it could offer in the way of nourishment. Some have to die in order that others may survive. Nature re-cycles many things. The snow was very deep and this made it difficult for the vixen to travel. Her determination kept her going for didn't she have cubs to feed?

She travelled for about a quarter of a mile and stopped. There, just ahead of her, in a small clearing, were three rabbits busily gnawing away at the bark of a tree — they, too, were having to improvise on their normal diet, though in order to ensure *their* survival it looked as though the tree would die quite soon, with all the bark stripped away by those and other rabbits. Eventually that would fall and decay, providing homes for insects, lichen and fungi before it enriched the soil, thus providing for the living trees and plants. The vixen dropped into a hunting stance and with ears flat against her head she crept forward, slowly, stealthily, like a domestic cat hunting a garden bird. For the cat it would provide a few moments 'sport' whether it caught the bird or not. For the fox its very survival depended on its skill and ingenuity. So she crept on, eyes fixed on the busy, chewing rabbits. Slowly she made her way towards them. They were quite unaware of her presence — hunger sometimes lessens the senses and certainly these rabbits showed no sign of either scenting or hearing the fox.

Gathering herself into a bundle of tensed muscles, positioning her hind legs into a good balancing posture, swaying from side to side she waited for the right second — and sprang. The rabbit, killed instantly by the sharp canine teeth of the fox never even knew what had happened, so exact had been the timing of the vixen. The other rabbits had bolted, but no matter. The dead rabbit was a large buck and would be a good two days supply of food.

Clamping her teeth round the prostrate form of the rabbit the vixen decided to return to the den and eat there. Now that she actually had the rabbit it did not seem to matter that the actual eating of it was to be put off until later. Half-carrying and half-dragging her kill she made her way back to the copse. Laying it down she stood, lifting her head and sniffing the air. She trembled. Sniffing again, she recognised that same fear-scent she had come across before giving birth. It was stronger than the last time. Cautiously, almost without moving, she stretched forward, peering over the mound of snow that had hidden her until then.

Ahead of her were three strange things, moving about, making sounds that could not possibly belong to her kind. Two were quite unrecognisable, but the third seemed to be an animal. She had not seen one before, but certainly it was covered in fur even if she did not know what it really was.

Caution caused her to shrink back, but as she did so, the animal gave a roar and in a split second was hurtling towards her. She was rooted to the ground momentarily, then instinct told her to run, run, run. She ran blindly, realising that it mattered not where she ran, just that she must keep away from this animal. Tripping and falling, panting, terrified, she continued. By this time she had no idea where she was and the terrain was strange to her. The snow covering the ground had also made familiar surroundings totally alien, but she struggled on, and on, and on. Around her she was aware of the danger cries of the sparrows and the crows, as they made their way to safety. Even though the vixen was calling on all her reserves of strength it was not enough, and when she could finally run no further she turned to face the enemy panting, shaking, teeth bared, lips drawn back from open mouth. She drew herself up as high as she could, the muscles contracting at the base of each hair on her body causing them to stand on end and 'double' her size. This valiant display of aggression was unheeded as with a final spring her enemy landed upon her, sinking its teeth into her shoulder as it did so. As she fell its teeth sank into her flesh yet again and this time one of them pierced her heart. She was dead. The hunter now hunted was no more.

The two men, for that is what they were, breathlessly approached the bloody scene. They leaned upon their sticks and grinning broadly congratulated themselves and their lurcher dog on a good morning's sport. Then one of them noticed this was a vixen with milk. It was obviously still feeding cubs and after a hurried discussion they decided to find the cubs. An ideal opportunity to give themselves and their dog some more pleasure. Slinging the body of the vixen over his shoulder one of the men led the way back, with the dog jumping up and down at the vixen. Finally they all arrived back at the spot where the chase had started. The dead rabbit still lay there, so the man picked that up, too. Not bad at all, so far, he thought.

By this time the lurcher was scratching frantically at the snow still covering the entrance to the den. One of the men pulled it away. They both listened. Yes, the dog had been right. It was the whimpering it had heard that had caused it to dig so frantically. There was something alive in among the tangled branches of the fallen tree. One of the men held the dog back while the other dug at the snow with his bare hands. Finally, having enlarged the entrance sufficiently to take his lean frame he disappeared from sight, emerging a minute or so later. He stood up and pointed to the pockets of his duffle coat. They were bulging and they were moving. Laughing, he pulled forth two fox cubs and threw them bodily towards the now whining dog. In a flash they too were dead. "'e deserves a reward." said the man. "After all, 'e not only caught the mother, 'e found these fer us, too! And 'im only six months old. 'E'll mek a good 'un, 'e will." And with that, thrust his hand into the other pocket, brought out the third cub and threw that to the dog.

Was the whole family to be destroyed? What made the man leave the last cub in his pocket will never be known, but he did and because of that I am able to write this story.

Walking back at a leisurely pace the two men decided that a call at the village 'local' would not come amiss. Also, it would be an opportunity to boast of their exploits of the morning and didn't they not only have the vixen and a rabbit but one of the cubs, live, as proof of their dog's prowess. Dropping the bodies at the door, and tying the dog to a post with a bit of string the two men walked in, winking at each other and nudging each other in anticipation of the glory that was to come their way and the attention they would receive while relating their story.

There was someone in that pub, though, who sat quietly in the background and listened with horror to the tale the men were telling. When one of them pulled the last cub out of a pocket and held it up for all to see, he could stand it no longer. Going up to them he asked them what they were going to do with this last one. This took quite a bit of consideration on their part, but then they decided that if no-one in there wanted it they might as well give it to the dog.

That man was called Bob Hughes. He left straight away, cradling the cub against him for warmth. When he arrived home, he related the tale to his wife and young daughter, put the cub in a cardboard box by the fire and they called it 'Foxy'.

FOXY AND SCRUFF

Foxy was hungry by now for it was a good six hours since he had his last feed from his mother, whom he was never to know or see again. All he knew was that hunger pangs made his tummy ache and he missed the warm closeness of his littermates. He lifted his blunt little nose up in a weak attempt to locate his mother. Fox cubs, like other young mammals have very few, if any, senses well developed at this age, but one sense was strong right from the moment of birth, and that was the scent of their mother's milk.

But where was his mother? He feebly threshed around, moving this way and that, seeking that comforting and essential smell. His cries became louder and urgent. Milk was not only necessary for him to grow but also to help retain his body fluid. Such small, young animals can die simply from dehydration.

Something moved towards him. Even though he could not yet see he was aware of some object. Then he was firmly grapsed round his middle. He had come across this man-scent before but was not yet to know that it belonged to his saviour, his good samaritan, his first friend in the alien world into which he had now come — Bob Hughes.

Gently lifting Foxy onto his lap Bob turned the little button nose towards him and gently pushed a medicine dropper into his mouth. Foxy fought against it, protesting loudly. It was hard and unfamilier and he wanted his mothers milk. So Bob put his little finger in the cub's mouth instead, thus forcing it open a little. Leaving his finger there he held the dropper up and dripped a small quantity of diluted evaporated milk onto Foxy's tongue. It trickled down his throat. It wasn't what he was used to but it tasted good. He thrust his head forward to seek some more of this pleasant liquid. Bob gently lowered the dropper into his eager mouth again, slowly removing his finger as he did so. The first important hurdle was over as the cub took its first, lifesaving, artificial feed of milk. Bob was immensely relieved as were his wife and daughter. His daughter was very young, too young really to understand what was going on, but even she knew that young animals, like young children, needed milk. Yvonne, Bob's wife, knew that she was going to have to help with the rearing of this young animal, for with Bob at work during the day, it would still require feeding.

She watched as Bob refilled the dropper and she smiled as the cub took its fourth re-fill. Gently she stroked the little tummy, now quite distended, and moved her finger up towards its head and then its nose. It would need to trust her scent, too, if they were to be successful in rearing this orphan of the wild. It stiffened a little and uttered a low growl as it sniffed her finger, but with a full tummy it was becoming decidedly sleepy, so that was its only objection before it was obviously in a sound, contented sleep.

Carefully lifting the tiny animal that was no bigger than his hand, Bob gently lowered it back into the cardboard box next to the fire. This was to be its new home for the next few weeks, since it needed constant warmth and regular meals of warm milk.

Going to the kitchen Bob returned with a small wad of moistened cotton wool which he gently rubbed over the sleeping cub's tummy. This was to simulate the licking of its mothers tongue because this served not only to wash the cubs but enabled them to defecate too. Voluntary passing of waste matter by the cub itself would not be fully functional for another week or so. By then its movements and struggles to begin stumbling around would provide the stimulus for this function to be performed by the individual cub. But until such time the end of each feed would be succeeded by the rubbing of its tummy with damp, warm, cotton wool!

Scruff, the family dog, was banished to the kitchen for the time being, for the cub had had enough upheaval for the moment, without being subjected to the inquisitive nose of a young, lively, rough coated Jack Russel Terrier!

During the night Bob got up and crept downstairs to warm some milk. The cub was peacefully sleeping, but took the proffered dropper, drank its fill and drifted back into a world of its own, where, in its mind, it may still have been in the den with its mother.

The next morning Bob went off to work with

instructions to Yvonne to be sure to feed the cub every four hours. And to be sure to remember to rub its tummy, too.

Scruff was, by this time, almost at the end of her tether, so much did she want to see what was going on in the other room. She whined and scratched at the kitchen door, putting her nose to the gap at the bottom and taking deep, scent-searching breaths, Yes, whatever it was they had in there was *most* interesting and even if it meant literally eating her way through the old wooden door she was *going* to find out what they had in there.

Because of her persistent determination, and also because there was a good possibility of having to re-hang a new door if Scruff continued the way she was, Yvonne relented and, putting her on a lead she allowed her into the lounge. Now that the door was actually open there was no need for rushing and hurrying any more. She had made her protest, now it was time to act in a dignified fashion.

Walking slowly and stiffly, Scruff approached the box. She was only a little dog so she had to stretch a bit to get her nose over the edge. This caused the box to move a little upon which the cub stirred. This movement made Scruff jump so she sat back on her haunches to have a think. Oh, well! Faint heart never won fair maid. She stepped forward again and nose-in-box inhaled the scent of the creature inside. It was a strange kind of scent but there were also scents she recognised. Those of her master and mistress. In that case it must be all right. She nuzzled it gently. The cub moved and tried to reach upwards to this familiar but different texture. Scruff licked the nose and the cub, unprotesting, lay back while the little terrier gently and firmly washed it all over!

The bond of friendship had been made. The instinct of the dog told her this was a helpless baby animal and brought forth the maternal feelings in the bitch that told her she must be gentle, but protective, too, of this little, warm, strange animal that lived in a cardboard box.

CHAPTER TWO — *LEARNING TO WALK*

FOXY SOON became acclimatised to the scents and smells of his new surroundings and settled into the routine of the Hughes' household. When he was twelve days old his eyes were fully open and he gazed about him trying to see this strange new world. He would never know that his real world should consist of grass and trees and freedom. Freedom to move about unrestricted in the copse and over the fields. Nor was he to know the pleasure of stalking and catching rabbits, toads and hedgehogs. He would not see the pheasants rise in a flurry ahead of him, alarming all the other birds into a twittering, shrieking cloud of flapping wings as they flew to safety.

On the other hand, Foxy would never need to go out in the dusk and spend his time during the dark hours of night looking for food and developing his hunting ability so that he could survive. The two men, and their dog, had made sure of that, when they first of all put the remaining cub in their pocket and secondly when they had handed him over to Bob Hughes. This fox cub was destined to spend his life in captivity.

As his ability to see became more pronounced, Foxy soon learnt to recognise the family who had adopted him, not only by sight but by scent as well. However, although he came to trust the human members of the family it was Scruff who gained his real affection.

During feeding times Scruff would sit watching and

when he was put back in his box she would rush over, short, stumpy tail wagging, and administer the washing ritual, sometimes placing her paw gently on top of Foxy, to be sure he kept still until she had finished.

When he was two and a half weeks old the cub was introduced to his first solid food. Had he still been in the wild it would have been towards the end of the fourth week that his mother would have regurgitated food for her offspring, for until they are about three weeks old, fox cubs have not started cutting their first set of teeth. However, his appetite was increasing and he was given some baby cereal mixed with milk. It was offered to him by finger to begin with and as he licked it off, obviously enjoying the taste, he soon progressed to licking it off a saucer. This extra food seemed to satisfy the cub's growing hunger and he slept between meals more contentedly.

Each day saw Foxy becoming stronger and when he was just over three weeks old he took his first, stumbling, rolling steps. By this time he was also staying awake a little longer each day and the Hughes family took great pleasure in handling him and having him out of his box and on the floor. In fact, the whole family would be on the floor, talking to and playing with, this delightful animal.

Like human babies, once a physical action is possible, it strengthens day by day and the end of the fourth week saw the cub actually *running*! Naturally it was not perfect, as one leg and then the other 'forgot' what it was supposed to do and the cub ended up on its nose .... but practice makes perfect and he soon got the hang of the rhythm of movement and he would run and bounce from one member of the family to another, little ears now pricked and upright and his rather nondescript tail carried merrily up and over his back. The natural flowing fall of the tail of the adult fox would come when he was about nine or ten weeks old.

By this time, too, he had started eating meat. The slight predicament of what to feed a fox on was solved when a little of Scruff's meat was offered to him and he nearly ate the finger it was on as well! So a nice easy routine was the order of the day and because he was now too big and active to stay in a cardboard box Foxy was allowed the freedom of the kitchen. Here he spent a lot of time playing with Scruff who put up with a tremendous amount as she allowed this little animal to pull her fur, bite her tail and hang on to her ears. Her nose was beginning to show signs of wear. Being black and shiny and so frequently pushed in his direction he found it too much of a temptation and would nip it, causing the dog to jump back with a squeak. Her nose never had time to heal and so, for the next few weeks, it developed scratches and scars that would have looked better on a prize boxer — the human kind, of course!

The daughter of the house loved handling Foxy but soon he became a little too rough. Not out of nastiness. It was simply that he was a fox cub, and fox cubs, like dog puppies, play with their teeth, so that soon she was gathering her share of scratches and scars, which is not a pretty sight on a little girl.

Bob spoke to his wife about it and a decision was reached. Foxy would have to start living outside in the garden shed and come into the house when the little girl was in bed and Bob was there to supervise what went on. So suddenly poor Foxy was again in a different place and for hours on end there was no-one to talk to him or play with him, even though, of course, he was given regular meals and drinks. It wasn't quite the same just coming into the house during the evenings and at weekends, but naturally, Bob had to put his daughter's welfare first and let us be fair .... Foxy was a wild animal. Only a baby wild animal, but nonetheless, a wild animal. Bob knew he would never forgive himself if the fox cub, now growing rapidly, leapt at his daughter's face, either in play or for any other reason. It is not every day one has a fox cub to look after so naturally one could not be expected to know how they developed or whether any instinct for survival came to the fore in the face of real or imagined danger.

At six weeks old Foxy was beginning to take on the true features of the adult. His muzzle had lengthened, his legs had grown longer and his fur, though still mainly 'puppy fluff' was beginning to develop the redness associated with the fox. What would be white when he was fully grown was still, however, a rather dirty grey. Had he still been living in the wild this lack of distinctive colouring would have helped to camouflage him no doubt.

The time that he was able to stay awake increased, though he still slept deeply and soundly having consumed each of the four meals a day. His teeth were totally through now and he could chew lumps of meat and pieces of biscuit. In fact, his diet was becoming quite varied, what with table scraps and titbits. His *most* favourite cereal was cornflakes, but *only* if they had sugar on and his other weakness, which he was to retain throughout his adult life, was chocolate! Now where a fox cub is ever likely to come across chocolate in the wild, I would not like to say. But chocolate he loved and so, because it was an aid in taming and training him, he was given it. Chocolate has sugar for energy and milk for calcium in it, so it was considered that on the whole it could only do him good — eaten in moderation of course.

Foxy eventually settled down into his new routine of living in the garden shed and coming in the house occasionally, but he was not to know that yet another change was shortly due to take place. Bob and his wife talked about the problem over and over again. It was becoming apparent that the facilities they could offer Foxy were not really good enough. They were, after all, living in a semi-detached house, with a moderate sized garden. The possibility of Foxy escaping as his agility increased had to be considered. And what were they going to do when he was adult? Where were they going to keep him? It would not be right or fair to condemn him for life to what they could offer him. Bob had saved him from certain death, reared him, weaned him — and loved him. That love for the cub now had to prove itself. It was agreed that somewhere else must be found for him. A sad decision but one that was ultimately to work out for the best.

Now, Bob often listened to the local radio station, Metro Radio, and every so often, about once a month, a girl called Sue Chambers was a guest for a 'phone-in programme to do with the training of dogs. She took calls, *via* the radio station, and answered them, over the air. The advice she gave always seemed sensible to Bob and he thought it would not be a bad idea to contact her, at her home 'phone number, to see if she knew anyone who might be interested in having this fox cub. He somehow felt that she cared about living creatures and would not suggest anyone unless she was certain they would be suitable.

So, one Friday in June, when Foxy was about ten weeks old, Bob telephoned Sue Chambers and told the tale of the fox cub. She listened with interest and amazement. He eventually came to the vital point. Did

A cautious approach to his first camera session!

Hold me tight!

she know *any*one who could offer a good, permanent home to the cub. Sue, having gone away to consult her husband, Tom, returned to tell Bob that *she* was willing to take him. Arrangements were made for Foxy to be collected the following day.

I am that Sue Chambers, and the following chapters of this book will, I am sure, enable you to understand my obsession and love for this most delightful creature as we developed an understanding, trust and mutual affection. This 'chance of a life-time' encounter gave me the opportunity to study the character and learn of the intelligence of this basically harmless country creature.

CHAPTER THREE — *THE MOVE TO 'HILLCREST'*

IN 1979 we moved from the hustle and bustle of Newcastle upon Tyne to a cottage in the country. A dream for the past five years had been realised as we were becoming more and more unhappy with life on the outskirts of the city, yearning for trees and grass and open country. Even living in Newcastle we had collected six dogs, four cats and a few rabbits and we felt the need for more space for our animals and ourselves.

When we moved it was one of the worst winters on record and the snow lay in six to ten foot mounds alongside the roads. However, with grit and determination we moved all our possessions the thirteen miles from Newcastle to Shotley Bridge. Three years later we had become quite comfortable having installed full central heating and Tom had built sheds and accommodation for the various animals we now had.

As the cottage stood in about an acre of ground the obvious choice of livestock were hens and ducks. Some of the hens had been 'inherited' with the house and the rest had been hatched by various hens determined to 'sit' on eggs. The ducks were Khaki Campbells. These proved to be very good 'layers' and they, too, hatched out young.

Then there was Perse. A most evil bird whose main aim in life seemed to be to grab hold of any person within reach of his beak and whack their legs with his wings. Perse is a gander and together with his two geese, he would parade round the field and garden terrorising anything that crossed his path, including the cats. These three birds are extremely good 'watchdogs' and apart from being ornamental the geese provide us with beautiful eggs from about February to May each year.

We acquired Nancy, the goat, the second year we were here. She had not been very well looked after but soon thrived on our love, attention, and any amount of grass she cared to consume. Even she repaid us by providing us with milk without being mated! Next on the list is Cyrus. He is a goat — yet another 'rescue' one! A sick and weak individual when he arrived, he too, thrived and six months later was a huge, stocky, bad-tempered addition to the stock. A bit like Perse, the gander, he was always on the lookout for some unwary person and would rush at them, hooking his horns under their legs and trying to lift them skyward. Just the sort of billy goat one reads about in children's story books where, opposite the writing there is a picture of some unfortunate person being flung heavenwards and the goat is snorting fire and fury! My two daughters, Sylvia and Philippa had their own small pets in the form of rabbits and guinea pigs. Visitors would be quite fascinated as they wandered round our little zoo.

The cats were an assortment of colours and sexes and one of *those* had been an unwanted stray, complete with litter of four beautiful kittens. We had three generations from that one queen. Our pride and joy, the dogs, have been left until the last. These were German Shepherds, formerly called Alsatians until the Kennel Club, with pressure put upon them by the Alsatian League of Great Britain, acted and officially put the name back to what they were originally called.

This breed I have owned and loved for over twenty

years. I have never had less than three at the same time and my two daughters were born into a life with German Shepherds. Not once have I had cause to regret choosing this breed and have found them to be loyal, extremely affectionate and totally trustworthy.

Anyhow, at the time Foxy was to come and live with us we had six German Shepherds, ranging in age from six months to six years and Tom, my husband, had a Rough Collie called Blue. This, then, was the life which Foxy was eventually to accept and love, but I will tell you more about that later.

I remember that Foxy was to be collected on a Saturday, because I had to leave Tom to travel over and get him as I had to go into Newcastle to take my Dog Handling Classes, so I could not go with him. Waking up really early that day I built the fox an indoor pen, where he could be confined and safe while he was still so young. We had a number of wooden pallets, given by a friend, and I used some of these to erect a largish pen with half of the top covered over. This was put in the utility room where it would be quiet for him, but where we could go and spend time with him as and when necessary.

I put newspaper on the floor of his pen, found some dishes for his food and water, put in a couple of cardboard boxes for him to hide in, if he wanted to, and then looked forward to coming home and finding him installed.

There was just one problem, though. What was I going to call him? Naming dogs was problem enough, but what was I going to call a fox? Yes, I know his name was Foxy, but, well — it is a bit obvious isn't it?

I decided that his new name would have to be similar to his old one to avoid confusing him and after much thought and deliberation settled on 'RACHZ', pronounced 'Rax'. It was different but would sound familiar to him.

I finished my classes that afternoon on the dot of 4.45 and rushed home to see our new and unusual addition to the menagerie.

CHAPTER FOUR — *RACHZ LEARNS TO TRUST*

WALKING QUIETLY into the utility room I peered into the pen. Rachz was inside one of the cardboard boxes and he was being ever so, ever so quiet. I put my hand towards the box, there was a rustle of straw and a low growl.

It was decided that he would be left to get used to his new surroundings undisturbed and I would try to win him round in the morning. That night we left him with food and milk and retired to bed. On Sunday morning I jumped out of bed nice and early so that I could see to the dogs and other animals and then spend time with Rachz. Those jobs done I climbed into the pen and sat there, talking to this little fox, saying anything and everything to let him know that he was safe and I was a friend. Each time I put my hand into his box he growled, but I persevered and at last got to the point where I actually touched him. He stiffened, growling, obviously still very frightened, but allowed me to rub his side gently for a few moments.

The thrill of touching him for the first time is still with me. His fur was soft, so very soft, and warm. I had made physical contact with this wild creature, and loved him, but I was not to know at that time how deep that love was to grow and how much I was to get in return. I spent three hours sitting in that pen, talking softly and gently. Like the majority of people, I had never kept a wild animal

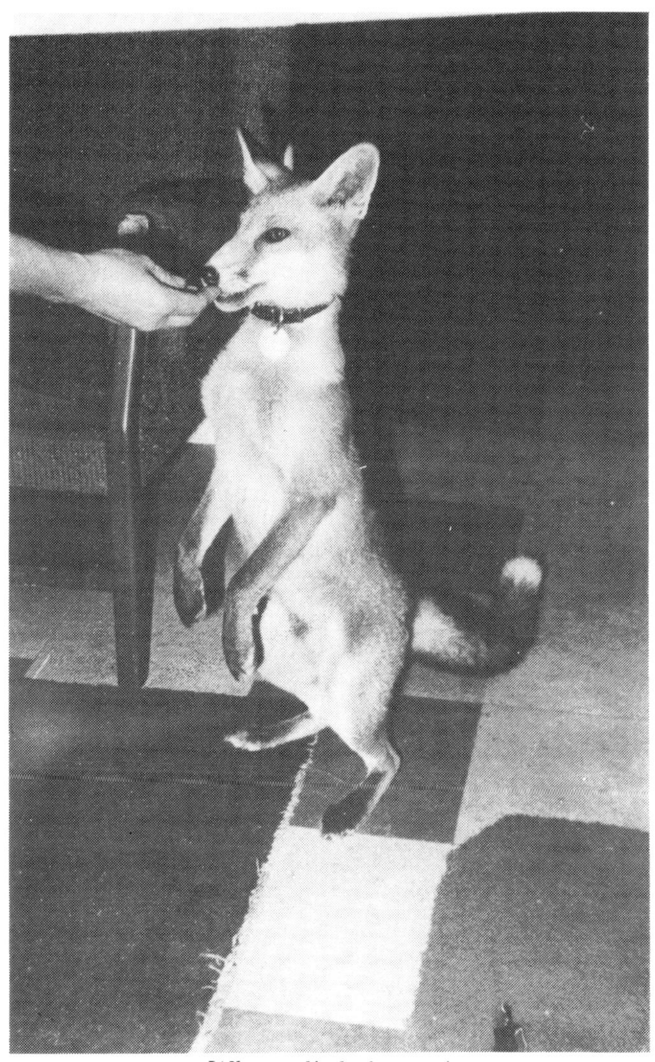

What a little beggar!

That looks tasty! Bajha gives Rachz confidence.

before, but one thing I did know, and that was that I had to have as much physical contact with him as possible, during the first few weeks of owning him, in order that he might come to know me and to trust me.

When you think about it, the whole experience of changing homes must have been really traumatic for Rachz. Dog puppies, domesticated over the centuries, have trouble for a few days adjusting to new homes when they are sold. How much more must this have affected the fox cub, with the instinct of centuries behind him to mistrust humans. And here he was with two homes in ten weeks. On the third day of his being here I was again sitting in his pen and all the talking I had done over the past two days was starting to pay off. His curiosity started to get the better of him and slowly he gained enough confidence to poke his face round the corner of his box.

What an enchanting face it was, too! Little button-nose and two bright eyes of the most beautiful golden amber all set into a wedge-shaped face with two of the most enormous ears that I had ever seen on such a young animal. Crawling cautiously out of his box he stretched his neck as far as he could in order to sniff me. I did not move, but spoke gently to him. He darted back inside but a few moments later was sufficiently composed to emerge again.

Soon he was coming out and walking round me, sniffing at my clothes and socks. I had taken my shoes off so that I did not bring any infection to him, for, of course, foxes are susceptible to the same diseases as dogs and he was not yet inoculated. Sudden movements still startled him and he still only accepted me touching him when he was in the safe confines of his box, but the initial breakthrough had been made.

Over the next few days he became more brave and would peer out of his box even when all four of us were gathered round to see him. One thing that did not cause any problems was his food. He ate four meals a day but for some strange reason just would not touch his breakfast cornflakes.

When I rang Bob Hughes to let him know how Rachz was I mentioned this and it transpired the solution was simple. He *did* love cornflakes — but only if they had sugar sprinkled on top! Henceforth it was cornflakes *with* sugar and he scoffed the lot. Whoever would have thought a fox could develop a sweet tooth!

The rest of his meals were varied. He liked cheese, eggs and milk and I also gave him sardines, cat food and dog food. In fact, he was fed in the same way I would rear a dog puppy. His other really favourite 'food' was chocolate as Bob Hughes had found. Hardly a diet for a fox but it was a very useful aid in taming him for he could *not* resist a chocolate drop offered to him between two fingers.

One thing I learnt very early on about foxes is that they are very quick to learn once they are over their initial fear. Rachz progressed in leaps and bounds and he quickly learnt to recognise myself and younger daughter, Philippa, for we were the two he saw most of. Soon, on hearing our voices he would rush out of his box, roll on his back and squeak in a high-pitched voice, wagging his tail and wanting his tummy tickled. Unless you really think about it, it is perhaps, not a very special thing for a young animal to do. But think more deeply and you come to one conclusion. That little fox had formed such a trust in us that he was prepared to adopt a position he would never do in the wild. Expose the soft underparts of his belly and throat. A predator would have ripped him open in a flash.

Yet here he was, not even one generation away from the wild open countryside, presenting us with a tummy to be tickled.

Day by day his trust and interest in us increased to the point that we were able to lift him out and bring him into the kichen for a run round. Little were we to know that was going to present us with a problem. As he realised that there was a world outside his pen he not only became more reluctant to go back into it, he started clambering *out* of it and we would come downstairs in the mornings to be met by a fox who had been out of his pen for hours and had amused himself by knocking plants off the window sill and pulling things out of the cupboard.

The answer, it seemed, was to put a wire lid on the top of his pen in order to confine him for a little while longer. To this he objected strongly and bit and clawed at it until we literally had to *tie* it down to keep him in.

The time had come for him to have a much larger pen, purpose-built just for him, outside. But before that he was to pay his first visit to my veterinary surgeon for his inoculations, because I believe in doing things properly or not at all.

The appointment was made, the special attenuated vaccine was obtained (the ordinary dog vaccine would have killed him) and I prepared myself for the trip from the country to Newcastle, with Rachz.

CHAPTER FIVE — *RACHZ VISITS THE VET*

THE APPOINTMENT was for 10.00 that morning and after seeing to all the other animals I prepared for the journey into Newcastle. Fortunately the Landrover had a partition between the driver's cab and the rear section, so I knew that once Rachz was in the back there was no way he could get out and be lost, even if I had the windows open in the front.

Rachz had been used to wearing a collar, but for safety I also put our name tag on — just in case. Then, clipping a dog lead to the collar I put him in the back of the Landrover. He scuttled round for a while and then settled into a corner, watching out through the rear window. As I drove along I watched him by glancing into the rear-view mirror. Cars that usually overtook me seemed to stay behind for longer than usual. No doubt they were doing 'double-takes' at the little face just visible in front of them!

The journey took half an hour and on arriving at my destination and parking as close to the surgery as possible, I slid back the glass partition and reaching through got hold of the lead attached to Rachz. With lots of encouragement I coaxed him into the front with me, then, tucking him under my arm, and making sure I had a good hold on his lead, I alighted and went into the reception area.

There were quite a few people there, with their dogs and cats and little cardboard boxes enclosing scuffling noises. They all, at one time or another, glanced my way, but no-one said anything. Isn't it funny how people *think* that what they are seeing is correct — but, no, it cannot be!

Eventually a gentleman came in and straight away knew it was a fox cub I had on my lap and we had quite a chat. The other people in the surgery suddenly came to life, having had their suspicions confirmed by this gentleman, and now, secure in the knowledge that they *had* thought right in the first place, they, too asked about Rachz and how I had come by him.

Soon it was our turn to go into the consulting room and placing the fox on the table I told the veterinary surgeon how I had come to own him. He was very interested — I don't suppose they have foxes in the surgery every day — and proceeded to give Rachz a thorough going over, sounding his heart and his lungs and peering down his ears and in his eyes.

Pronouncing him a fit and healthy animal he then prepared the vaccine.

I was rather dubious as to how Rachz would accept having the needle stuck into him and had come prepared with a pair of really thick and heavy gardening gloves. I did not have to worry. Not only was the vet very quiet and gentle with him, but Rachz did not bat an eyelid when he was given his innoculation. I remarked to the vet that he had probably behaved himself better than some of his canine counterparts. The reply was a vigorous agreement!

Knowing I was keen on training dogs Ian Winter, the vet, then asked if I intended training Rachz. I replied that I would attempt only two things, to teach him to 'sit' and 'come'. What was most important, I told him, was that the fox grew tame and that it was time spent with him that was going to achieve this. We had already discussed the possibility of setting the fox free, back into the wild, but this had been discounted, because, in the vet's opinion, he had been so 'humanised' from such an early age, it would probably be cruel to set him free as an adult. More important, perhaps, was the fact that once this fox met our dogs and grew to know them and relate to them, he would lose his mistrust of dogs and one day might die because of it.

So that day it was decided Rachz was to spend his life in captivity. But he was a male fox and of course, the time for mating would come with the autumn months. Rachz with his instincts unfulfilled, would be an unhappy, possibly destructive and probably bad-tempered animal. The obvious action was to have him castrated. This would have the effect of 'dimming' his mating instinct, would prevent him calling for a mate and all round would be the best possible thing under the circumstances. All this I wholeheartedly agreed with. According to Ian Winter foxes mature early, so I was told to make an appointment to have him castrated when he was about six months old.

Rachz received a friendly scratch behind the ear from Ian and as we left he wished me 'good luck' with the fox. Climbing back into the Landrover, with Rachz duly put into the back again, we made our way home.

Vastly relieved that the whole operation had gone without trouble I pulled up on our driveway and carried out the last part of my expedition — transferring Rachz from the car back into his comfortable and familiar pen in the utility room. He settled down with a drink of milk, none the worse for his ordeal and the next time I looked in on him, he was fast asleep. The vaccine would produce immunity over the next two weeks, from the major dog diseases and then I would have the next part of his education to look forward to. He would be introduced to the dogs.

NOW THAT he had been vaccinated it would be safe for him to mix with the dogs and cats. Prior to this I had discussed my intentions with various friends. Without exception they thought it would be interesting, but, of course, I would have to watch the dogs because it would be in their instinct to kill him! Who was I to argue? I had never had a fox before so was quite unaware of *how* each would react to the other . . . I decided that the first to be introduced would be Panda. He was six years old, very sensible and well-trained and quite used to meeting all sorts of dogs and cats. However, as he had not met a fox before I decided to play safe and put him on a lead, so that I would have full control over him should anything go wrong.

With Rachz in the kitchen I quietly entered with Panda. Telling him to 'down' I sat on a chair, holding his lead and watched and waited.

Rachz came creeping up to him, interested, but wary, and proceeded to sniff Panda all over. Satisfied that this large and hairy dog was harmless he then decided it would be fun to play with bits of him.

Panda's feet were the first to be pulled at . . . then his tail! Panda looked at the fox, then at me. Puzzlement covered his face, and he shifted uneasily at the fox's attentions. After all, not even his kennel-mates took liberties like that with him! I told him what a good boy he was and he wagged his tail. An unwise move, that. For on

Can't catch me! Rachz pops up between Bajha and Minstrel.

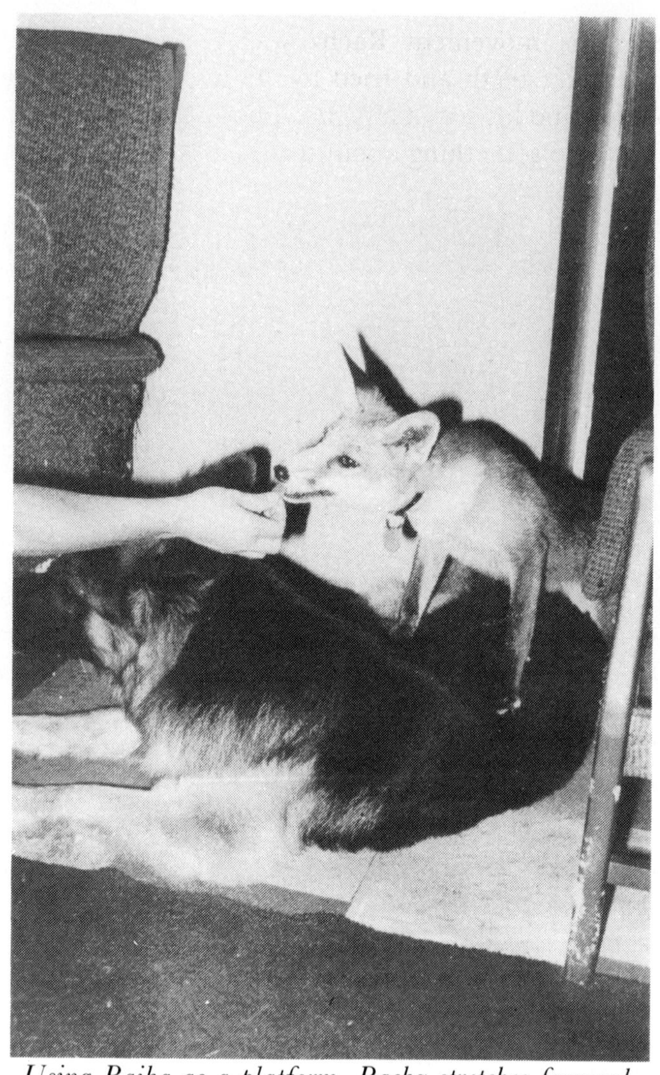

*Using Bajha as a platform, Rachz stretches forward
for a chocolate drop.*

seeing the movement Rachz was upon it, grabbed it between his teeth and tried to run away with it! Panda stood up and looked at me, pleading with me, through his eyes, do do something about this funny little animal that liked tails.

The time had come, I thought, to call this first meeting to a halt, before Rachz really got carried away and hurt Panda. I wagged my finger at Rachz and told him he was bad, in a cross voice. He responded by leaving go of Panda's tail, running under a chair and 'grinning' at me! Praising Panda again, I then took him back into the lounge. He was relieved, I could tell, to be away from that biting fox cub, but he had behaved well, and I was pleased with him.

The next dog to have the pleasure of meeting our fox was Bajha. He is another German Shepherd with a long coat. Although this extreme length of coat is a genetic fault, I deliberately breed for it as it is so attractive. Bajha was one of Panda's grand-sons and two and a half years old. Slightly larger than Panda he, too, had a lovely bushy tail, and after the last experience of bushy tails, I knew what was going to happen to *this* one.

Even though the introduction to Panda had gone without incident I put Bajha on the lead and took him into the kitchen.

The reaction from the fox was totally different to when he met Panda. On seeing Bajha he ran up to him and raised himself up on his hind legs to sniff the dog's neck. Then he started rolling on his back and squeaking! The same sort of pleasurable squeak until then reserved for us humans. He ran round the kitchen, coming up to Bajha periodically to sniff him. There was certainly something about Bajha that appealed to him.

When I told Bajha to lie down, Rachz settled down a bit and upon examining the dog more closely, he discovered his tail! Now whether Bajha had a less sensitive tail than Panda I do not know — but he actually allowed this fox to pull, and pull and pull, without showing any signs of discomfort or annoyance. Rachz took full advantage of this and when he had finished with the tail he started on the feet. Now his teeth were very sharp and although Bajha accepted having his tail pulled, feet were a different matter. As Rachz nipped at his feet, Bajha drew them under his chest to get them out of the way, eventually getting up altogether and making for the nearest chair. We had two old chairs in the kitchen that the dogs were allowed to lie on.

Jumping up on the chair he curled himself into a ball and foolishly left his forelegs dangling over the edge. Rachz did not miss this opportunity and nipped at them. Bajha learnt quickly and thereafter, when lying on a chair, would immediately tuck his feet under himself!

Rachz seemed unconcerned by the dogs, once he had got over his initial introduction. In fact, he seemed to be absolutely enamoured of them. Perhaps they reminded him of Scruff! I allowed Bajha to stay in the kitchen a little while longer, so that I could watch both of them enjoying each other's company, then back Bajha went, into the lounge and Rachz went back into his pen.

Thoroughly pleased with the way everything had turned out I thought back to the warnings about foxes and dogs. Thinking about it deeply I could come to one conclusion only. All my dogs are obedience-trained to mix and be sociable with humans, dogs and cats, and to ignore any animosity shown to them by other animals. They were used to coming everywhere with me and coming into contact with other peoples' animals. This little fox was, then, to them, just one more puppy that bit their tails and chewed their feet. That they had been trained to behave, from an early age had, I am sure, made these initial introductions so successful. The other dogs would meet him at a later date, I decided, since three of them were very young and still somewhat rough in their play. An active, exuberant, young dog might frighten Rachz and I knew I would have to bide my time. There would be ample opportunity for Rachz to play with the two that had been introduced to him, though I felt Bajha was going to be a special friend to him. This initial judgement would prove to be true, but you will hear more about that later on in this book.

The next animals to introduce him to were — the cats!

CHAPTER SEVEN — *RACHZ MEETS THE CATS*

AT THE time we had five cats. The oldest was a black tomcat called T.C. The initials stood for 'That Cat' for when he was a kitten he was always up to something that he shouldn't be and one or another of us seemed constantly to be saying 'What's that darned cat up to now?'

Next in line was Cleo — a cat rescued from certain death having been taken to the RSPCA kennels while I was doing a stint there. She and her newborn kittens were found in a coalhouse one cold November morning with nothing between them and the damp floor but two rotting sheets of newspaper.

Unfortunately, even though exhaustive efforts were made, instigated by me, to find her owners, we were unsuccessful, and since there was just no more room to house yet another cat it was unfortunately to be a case for the lethal box. Yet somehow this cat lovingly curled round her four kittens had luck on her side. For since I had become so involved with them the few hours they were on the premises, even in that short time an attachment had formed and I got permission to take her and her kittens home with me that evening. We put her and her babies in the airing cupboard in the bathroom, gave her food and drink and left her to settle for the night.

She was a doting, protective and loving mother to her kittens who all turned out to be beautiful young cats by the time they were six weeks old. I had lined up responsible homes for all of them, including Cleo. Unfortunately, or fortunately, depending on how you choose to look at it, the gentleman who was prepared to take Cleo arrived to collect her two months after her kittens had gone — by which time she had grown attached to me, and so she stayed.

Over the next couple of years she had many more beautiful kittens. Word got round so that I always had a 'waiting list' of people wanting one of Cleo's kittens. All the prospective owners had to agree to have the kitten inoculated and neutered, before I would agree to them having one, AND they had to pay a nominal sum of money towards the rearing of them. When I decided that she had had enough kittens, we kept one from her last litter and had her spayed.

The kitten we kept was called Kizzy. She eventually produced a litter of kittens, unfortunately born by caesarian section. After they were reared we had Kizzy spayed, too.

This litter of hers was something of a worry. Due to the anaesthetic the kittens were practically lifeless at birth and had to be rubbed before a warm fan heater to get them going. This took nearly an hour. When they were nine days old I noticed that their tails had shrivelled almost to the root! Convinced they would have to be put to sleep I rushed them to the vet who promptly gave each of them a local anaesthetic and cut their tails off! It transpired that because the blood supply had taken so long to circulate round their bodies at birth, the extremeties (i.e. tails and ears) had been starved of a blood supply and 'died'.

The fact that they were 'tail-less presented us with problems, for people were reluctant to take on a cat with no tail. Don't ask me why. The kittens were perfectly healthy in all other respects. I even devised simple tests to check that there had not been any 'brain damage' due to the blood and therefore the oxygen supply in the bloodstream, not getting to the brain as quickly as it should. They were normal in every way. Except for those tails — or lack of them.

However, we eventually managed to find three of them loving, caring homes. The fourth, a little black and white tom was the one no-one wanted, and so he stayed with us. In fact, my daughter, Philippa, asked if she could have him as a birthday present. So he became 'her' cat and she called him Minstrel.

He has turned out to be one of the best cats we have ever had. Charming, playful, affectionate, afraid of nothing and with great character, where people thought it strange, on meeting him, that he had no tail, WE began to find ourselves thinking it strange that other cats HAD tails! Of course he would have been quite normal in the Isle of Man, where tails are not worn by the best Manx cats.

Then Pampas arrived. Originally he belonged to some people we knew but the lady suffered a bad fall and had to undergo intensive and lengthy hospital treatment. Worried that she would not be able to look after him she asked us to give him a home. He was a beautiful Blue Persian aged eighteen months when he came to us. Being an easy-going and pleasant cat he spent a lot of time lazing about on the chairs.

At that time Minstrel was about eight weeks old and we would often find him snuggling in among the long coat of Pampas, being licked clean, with the large cat's paws wrapped round him.

That was the beginning of a remarkable friendship that was to last until Pampas had to be put to sleep three years later from complications arising from a urinary problem. Up to that time Minstrel could always be found where Pampas was, whether it was chasing birds in the garden or curled up together, each washing the other, on a chair by the fire.

When Pampas died Minstrel was devastated. He sat in front of the fire every evening making plaintive mewing noises that went on, and on, and on. It was pitiful to hear and see and there was nothing that any of us could do to ease his suffering. He eventually settled down a bit, but even six months after his friend had gone there would still be the occasional lapse and the mewing would commence again. I don't think that little cat will EVER get over the loss.

Anyway, that was in the future, for we still had Pampas when Rachz was to meet the cats for the first time.

T.C., Cleo and Kizzy were non-starters. None of them would even stay in the kitchen while Rachz was there. With a great deal of spitting, snarling and extremely annoyed expressions, they, in turn, made for the door that opened into the lounge. There was NO WAY they were even going to TRY to get to know Rachz.

Pampas and Minstrel were an entirely different matter. We decided to bring both of them into the kitchen together. Placing them on one of the chairs we sat down to watch. At first they were unaware that there was anything else in the kitchen as Rachz had hidden himself under one of the chairs.

Both cats curled up on the chair and proceeded to wash each other. Slowly Rachz poked his nose out from under the chair. He edged himself forward just a little bit and sniffed the air. The cats ears twitched but they carried on with their wash and brush-up. Rachz eased himself out and stealthily crept forward to where the cats were. They were still oblivious of him. Then, without moving his body forward any more Rachz stretched and stretched his head forward until he could sniff at one of the cats. It made a purring noise, as they often do when we stroke them in passing, and looked over its shoulder.

Suddenly, with a hiss and a swear, stiff legs and all their hair on end, the cats leapt to the top of the chair. This sudden noise and movement gave Rachz an equally bad fright and he shot away from them and hid in a corner, ears flat against his head and his beautiful amber eyes wide with fright.

The cats' attention was now focused totally on this alien creature, but curiosity getting the better of them, they stayed where they were and observed.

Gradually the cats settled themselves and so did Rachz. Minstrel decided that he was going to take a closer look at the fox and carefully climbed down. Walking stiffly and with a sideways movement he approached Rachz. He was on his guard and as Minstrel came closer he opened his mouth wide, flattened his ears against his head again, and arched his back. Undeterred, Minstrel strode determinedly on. Soon he was close enough to sniff Rachz. It was interesting watching them as Rachz responded and sniffed at Minstrel. One could almost feel the tense atmosphere relax as each began to realise that the other meant no harm. Minstrel turned to walk away, satisfied with his exploration of the fox. As he did so Rachz followed and made tentative grabs, with his teeth, at the stump that once was the cat's tail. Minstrel turned to look at him, batted him with his paw and then continued walking.

It was clear that Rachz had begun to realise this was another playmate, another friend. His facial expression had changed from that of a frightened animal to one with mischief all over it.

Pampas, meanwhile, was sitting on the chair taking it all in but had decided not to get involved.

Within a short time after that the fox and the cat were playing with each other. Balancing on their hind legs they would play at shadow-boxing, then one would run, only to be followed by the other. With one under a chair and occasionally sticking its nose out, the other would creep round behind and grab at a hind leg, or a tail. It was fascinating to watch these animals together.

First we had introduced the dogs, who *could* have been a natural enemy, to the fox. Then we had introduced the fox to the cats, who might well have been caught by a really wild fox, and ended up as its dinner! Yet, here we were, dogs and fox and cats mixing, admittedly with supervision from us, not only tolerating each other, but actually playing.

When Rachz went up to see Pampas who was still perched on his chair, the cat stuck its paw out at him and swore, but remained where he was. Rachz, having found a playmate in Minstrel, left Pampas and returned to his games with the other cat.

As we had done with the dogs, we let them be together for a little while longer and then removed the cats from the kitchen. All the necessary introductions had been made. We were more than happy with the outcome and there would be plenty of time in the future, for them to meet again and play some more. A whole new world was opening for Rachz and the next stage of his education was to be really interesting. He needed more exercise and he needed fresh air. He needed to run and play and jump about. The next stage was to teach him to accept being on a lead and learn to go outside into our field. There I would be able to allow him a great deal more room to stretch his legs. He would be able to see interesting things and smell interesting smells. Most important of all, he would pick up the scent of his 'home' which would mean that if he ever got lost and wanted to find his way home, he would be able to do so.

CHAPTER EIGHT — *THE GRASS UNDER HIS FEET*

RACHZ did not like the look of the big world outside the back door and he pulled backwards on his lead when I attempted to walk him out. I was a bit taken aback for I had expected him to be really keen to explore when given the opportunity to do so. Had he been a dog puppy I would have ignored his reluctance and with lots of encouragement and happy words pulled him towards me and praised him for being so clever!

What was I to do here? It was obvious that he would panic if I forced him against his will. And panic would cause him to take a backward step as far as his trust in me was concerned. I decided that compromise was the answer, so I picked him up and carried him slowly from the back door, past the conservatory, down the six steps leading to the dogs' kennels and runs and through the gate into the bottom field. The 'bottom field' is in fact no different from the 'top field' since they are both part of the long strip of land that runs alongside the house. But sectioning them verbally in this fashion at least enabled to know *which* part of the field was being mentioned and saved arguments. So the 'top field' was the part from the fence to the dog-run and the 'bottom field' was the rest, from the dog-run down to the old stone wall. In total about half an acre.

Once I had reached a quiet and secluded spot I put the fox onto the grass. He sniffed the ground and scratched at

the soil with one fore-foot. Slowly he walked around,
taking in the scents of the grass, the soil and the air. In the
wild he would have been used to all this from the age of
about six weeks but, of course, with his first world
consisting of floors and carpets and walls, all this was as
strange to him as it would have been were the situations
reversed and he had been used to open fields and grass,
and then taken into the confines of a house.

It was quite obvious that he was enjoying this new
experience. Talking to him all the while I followed where
he led as he became more brave and ventured further
afield. After about ten minutes I decided that he had had
enough for one day, so I picked him up and carried him
back to the house.

When I neared the conservatory I put him on the
ground to see what he would do. He looked about him and
then pulled towards the wall of the house. Clinging to the
wall he lowered his body and, following the wall, slunk
forward, ears pricked for any danger, until he came to the
back door. Once there, he shot inside with just a quick
glance over his shoulder to make sure there was just me
behind him. From now on, I thought, I must take him
outside at least four times a day, so that he would gain
confidence and could enjoy his exercise to the full.

It was more than a week before he would walk out of
the back door of his own accord, but he *always* walked back
to the house from the spot at which I had put him down on
his first time out.

There came the time, too, when he saw his first
chicken. The instinct was there, even though he did not
acutally know what to do about it. For when he saw the
bird he immediately dropped into a hunting posture, with
ears flat against his head and his eyes fixed on this

obviously appetising object. With a sudden movement he shot forward being restrained from chasing it by the lead. Immediately he realised he could go no further it was as if he could not care less about the bird. He turned away and his mind turned to other things, like digging a hole.

The longer we had him the more he ignored the birds when I had him out on the lead. Of course, I did not tempt fate, and made sure I was always a good distance from the geese, hens and ducks. I did think, however, that were he not restrained by the lead, he would have chased, caught and killed. The wild instinct was obviously there, despite the fact he had not only never had the opportunity to learn from his mother, he had never even had raw meat to eat. How deeply that instinct was ingrained in him I was not to know until, due totally to my complacency, he did get one of my hens. Tragic though this was it had a most astonishing aspect. You will read about this incident later on.

By now it was July and the following weeks were to see me and my fox spending a lot of time walking in the field. I would take him out in the morning, after the dogs had been out in their runs and the other animals had been fed and watered, and he would spend time exploring. I discovered he preferred the bottom field to the top field. Perhaps because that was a more secluded area, being away from the main road, and he felt safer. The bottom field had been full of large grass hummocks when we moved into 'Hillcrest' but over the past two years I had dug all but one of them out and filled the gaping holes with soil. Grass had long since grown over these bare patches.

The hummock that I left had a useful purpose. It was very comfortable to sit on during what spare minutes I had in the long summer days. A most unique hummock in fact. The interior filling of the most luxurious armchair could not have equalled the comfort of that hummock. And so it stayed and Tom also had strict instructions not to do away with it either. Rachz took an instant liking to this interesting clump of grass and during his runs in the field would frequently go over to it and lie all over it, pushing his nose into the interesting softness of it and breathing deep breaths. Perhaps he could smell the little insects that were bound to be living deep inside.

One day, while having his morning constitutional, Rachz displayed an incredible trait. He suddenly looked at me, then ran to where his long lead was trailing on the ground, got hold of it between his teeth and pulled. It was exactly the sort of thing a young dog puppy would do. However, by this time his adult teeth were through and I was a little worried that he might cut through the soft and supple leather and that would be the end of Rachz because he would be away across the fields. So I decided to divert his attention and picked up a small twig. Waving it at him I pretended to throw it. He immediately let go of the lead and darted towards me never taking his eyes off the twig. I threw it and as it landed in the long grass, among all the other little twigs, Rachz ran after it. It was clear, when he arrived at the point where it had fallen that he was not sure where it was. He had marked the area but was not sure of the exact spot. To my amazement he sniffed at the other twigs that littered the ground and eventually *picked up the one I had thrown!* I repeated the twig throwing with a new piece. The same happened again and he quartered the ground until he found the one *with my scent on.* It was quite obvious this was what he was doing. A trained dog could not have done better in competitive obedience scent discrimination! The scent with which I had impregnated

Bahli watches as Rachz has a good sniff at the hummock.

What's down there? Rachz on one of his digging sprees.

the twig during the couple of seconds it was between my fingers was sufficient for him to find it.

It was the same with fallen leaves. Sometimes he marked the spot where it fell and went straight to it. Other times he would search until he came across the one with my scent on. I was left in no doubt whatsoever about his ability to recognise my scent among all the other scents on the ground. I felt privileged to have discovered and observed this remarkable feat.

The novelty of Rachz never wore off and I was constantly thinking of ways to make these little treks interesting for him. Alongside the trees that ran all the way down the side of the field there were the remnants of rabbit burrows, long ago vacated after a particularly heavy spate of rain flooded them. Rachz took great delight in digging out these holes and I allowed him to do this since he was a fox, and after all, and I felt he needed to do a bit of digging now and again. It would help develop his muscles and was a form of strenuous exercise that would tire him out so that his time in the pen would be more bearable.

As he dug, his little face would disappear down the hole, to emerge covered in particles of soil, his eyes alight with enjoyment. At times like these I would feel such a twinge of guilt that he was a wild animal kept captive. I often wished that I could just let him off his lead in order to watch him take off across the farmer's field to the little wood in the distance: free and living a natural existence. I was sad because I knew this could never be. He would be free, yes, but would he be able to hunt for his food? Would he recognise predators? Would he know how to run and dodge and hide in the face of danger. He might have had

some latent instinct, but he had never had the experience
of being taught by his own kind.

Rachz was destined to spend his life in captivity and
because I was instrumental in this I made a silent vow. I
would have to love this fox enough to give him the
maximum amout of time I could spare and I would have
to do my best to keep him happy. It was not difficult to
make this promise to him. Quite simply, I loved him. I
loved him when I looked at him and I loved him when I
touched him. Without wishing to sound dramatic, it was
the kind of love that would have given me the courage to
defend him against any danger. I would have been
prepared to risk my life for him. It was a strange,
unexplainable kind of love.

Now that he was getting bigger he needed more space
during the time he was penned. The time had come for me
to request Tom to build him a pen and sleeping quarters
outside. This way he would be able to see the outside
world and sit in the sun, or have a nap. Also, with more
space for him to run and jump I would not be obliged
actually to take him outside so often for exercise.

CHAPTER NINE — *THE HOUSE THAT TOM BUILT*

T OM WORKED long and hard at his job and was frequently too tired in the evenings to do anything except relax and unwind; so I had to bide my time and wait until a weekend for him to make a start on the new quarters for Rachz.

Always on the lookout for anything that might 'come in useful' we had acquired a very large crate that had housed a big piece of machinery during transportation. This, then, turned on its side, was to be the pen area. First it had to be securely anchored against the fearsome winds that sometimes swept our hillside home. Two large posts were sunk into the ground and the crate was bolted to these.

Before a wire front could be put on it a sleeping area had to be devised and this turned out to be a most ingenious affair. Tom built a 'double skinned' wooden box. Between the 'skins' were layers of glass fibre left over from insulating the conservatory roof. This box was then set next to one end of the crate and a hole was made in the side of the crate, about two feet up, to make an access to the sleeping area. A ledge was then fixed between the box and the crate so that Rachz would be able to jump up onto the ledge and then go through the hole into his bed!

A removable roof was then made for the sleeping area to facilitate cleaning it out. It was covered in roofing felt; a paddlock was fitted to secure the roof to the box and there

it was — a purpose made 'den'! The front of the crate was
then covered threequarters of the way across with strong
wire netting. That just left Tom to think out an idea for the
remaining quarter because *we* had to have access to the
crate to clean out the floor area. In the end he boarded up
the bottom third and then made a sort of door that
dropped into place to fill in the remainder. This was kept
in place by fixing two staples on either side and running a
strong steel rod between them.

Calling me over Tom suggested I had a go at removing
the door while he was there, for that was to be the way I
would be putting food in for the fox. What a struggle it
was! Everything was certainly strong and firmly fixed! I
ventured to put forward a suggestion. One ventures
suggestions with Tom! 'Why don't you', I said, 'make a
little hatchway affair, set into the door, that I could just lift
up, pop his food in and close afterwards?'

This idea was accepted and very soon there was my
little 'serving hatch' all nicely hinged and kept shut with
the help of a hasp and staple and, to prevent escape of the
proposed occupant, a padlock.

There were just two more things to attend to. Plenty of
straw in his bed and some long logs of wood in the pen area
so that he would be able to jump and climb. With the logs
suitably arranged and plenty of sawdust on the floor it was
now ready for Rachz.

I was really looking forward to introducing the fox to
his new place so when it was finished we all gathered
round to see how he would take to it. It was a huge success.
He had a good look round and climbed up the logs. Then,
jumping down, he made his way to the ledge that gave him
access to his bed. Putting just his forelegs onto the ledge he
peered cautiously into the darkness. He was undecided

about this but, as usual, curiosity overcame apprehension and soon he was rustling around in the straw. After making sure that the two padlocks were secure we left him to enjoy his new home.

Even though he was now away from the house, I was still able to see a lot of him, because his pen was situated right next to the dog kennels and runs, so that each time I put the dogs out I was able to see and speak to Rachz. Occasionally I would unlock his 'serving hatch' and pushing my arm through would scratch the presented upturned tummy. While I was doing this Rachz would make those little pleasurable squeaking noises that I have mentioned before. I was happy that Rachz was happy and able to move around more freely. He also had the added pleasure of being able to see the dogs when they were in the run.

He could also see the hens and ducks. The hens in particular were quite unafraid of him and I would often go out to find them pecking round the wire of his pen for any fallen bits of food. At intervals a paw would poke through the wire in an effort to catch one of the hens!

I thought that the sight of so many hens so close to him might be too much and that he would rush around in a frenzy. But he never did. He either sat observing them or stuck a paw out at them.

Often I would find him curled up on one of the logs, basking in the warm summer sunshine. He seemed to be reversing a fox's way of life for he spent much of the day in his pen and presumably most of the night asleep. I still gave him as much of my company as I could, but felt less obligated to actually take him out for exercise. However, I did persevere with having him out in the field once each day — more because it gave me the opportunity of close contact with him, than the fact that he actually *needed* it. It was shortly after he was installed in his new quarters that I decided he should have the company of one of the dogs when I had him out in the field.

Bahli and Rachz relax after a game of catch-me-if-you-can.

Bahli peers inquisitively at Rachz – what is he going to do now?

CHAPTER TEN — *RACHZ RUNS WITH THE DOGS*

I DECIDED that since Rachz got on so well with Bajha that he should be the first to come out in the field with the fox. There was no way of knowing beforehand how the dog would react to the fox out in the open, particularly bearing in mind that Rachz ran and jumped and played when outside. Would the dog remain calm? Or would the situation bring forth a latent instinct to hunt? I knew that Bajha would drop on command so I felt that the situation would be under control before it had an opportunity to get out of hand.

Taking Bajha with me to the field I opened the hatch to the pen, attached the lead to Rachz's collar and he clambered through, squeaking and wagging his tail at the sight and smell of his friend. Bajha raised his tail and wagged it, too. So far, so good.

Once on the ground the fox, obviously ready for some exercise, decided the first thing he would do was run. He ran, I ran, Bajha ran. We all ran up the field. Once he reached the grass hummock, Rachz stopped, crouched, waited for Bajha to catch up and then pounced upon him. The dog looked a bit startled, but stood quite still. Rachz bit his front legs, bit his neck and then hung on to his tail. Bajha batted him with a paw at which the fox took off, running in circles with the dog following. Every so often the fox would suddenly stop, turn and run in the opposite direction, obviously totally unafraid that the dog was chasing him and treating the whole thing as a great game, which it was, for I observed the dog closely and could tell that his chasing was not a 'hunting to kill' but simply a game of tag. Occasionally, during the chase the dog would be running alongside the fox and not once was there the slightest hint of aggression.

Rachz however, was not as restrained with his teeth as the dogs had been taught to be and I could see that when he nipped Bajha he was really sinking his teeth into the flesh. So in order that the dog's patience and good manners were not pushed to the limit I called a halt and put the fox back into his pen. There would be plenty of time for him to have further games with the dogs. It was so nice to see him enjoying the company of another animal.

While he got on well with the dogs in the house and outside, the cats were a different matter. Indoors he would play with Minstrel and tantalise Pampas but if he spotted them walking in the field he would stop and fix his gaze upon them and there was no mistaking the intention in his mind. They were obviously potential 'supper' material.

I found that quite interesting, and having thought about it came to the conclusion that when he was outside he became far more excitable, with the feel of grass under his feet and the fresh air about his head. This excitability overrode his control, which operated in the house, simply because there was so much more space in the field. It was around this time, too, that I found him becoming a little difficult to manage, for when I picked him up to put him back in his pen he would resist for all he was worth, often biting or scratching me in the process. He also took to uttering low growls, which I did not worry about myself, for I was sure he would never attack me, but I was just a little concerned. I could foresee the time when it would be

Rachz investigates an interesting scent.

*Ducks and a goat in the background
and Rachz remains totally relaxed.*

impossible for me to get him back in his pen and the longer this took the more upset and on the defensive he would become. Each time I came indoors, dripping blood from scratches and bites, Tom would ask me if I still wanted to keep him. This was a silly question really, for even though there were a few handling problems I still loved that fox. I also knew somehow that he would not respond to cross words, as a dog would learn to do, and stop biting. All I could do when he started acting up was to talk to him in a soothing, loving tone, to try and keep him as calm as possible.

There was no way I was going to give up on this little fox just because of a few bites. After all, I was permanently covered against tetanus, because of my job, so had nothing to fear on the infection front! He was now six months old and Ian Winter had said they matured early. Obviously this was partly the cause of his erratic behaviour, the other part being that he just did not like going *back* into his pen, so the time had arrived when I would have to make an appointment for his castration operation.

CHAPTER ELEVEN — *OPERATION*

RACHZ started behaving rather strangely over the next few days. He shook his head periodically and rubbed the side of this face against the tree stump in his pen. Having seen this head-shaking in dogs and knowing it to be associated with ear trouble I was a little concerned. Not because it might be an ear infection — they are usually minor ailments and clear up rapidly with ear-drops — it was because medication might be required that I was worried, for how was this fox going to react? Would it set him back in any way?

When four days had passed and he was still obviously uncomfortable, I rang the vet and made yet another appointment with Ian.

The day before the appointment my daughter, Philippa, came to tell me that one of her rabbits had a runny nose. I vaguely remembered having read somewhere that rabbits could suffer 'snuffles' and that they needed antibiotics to rectify the situation, so I rang the surgery yet again, to say that I would be bringing a rabbit, too! They must have thought me quite mad, bringing a rabbit *and* a fox together.

The following day, rabbit confined in a cage and Rachz in the rear of the Landrover, I set off with my unlikely cargo. When we arrived I had to decide how to get both animals into the waiting room. Rabbit went first and his cage was placed under one of the chairs. Then I went back for Rachz. The problem of getting them both back into the Landrover I would deal with after they had been seen. The fox was first on the table and when I had explained to Ian about his head-shaking and rubbing he plugged in his surgical instrument to have a good look in his ear. I had my doubts about the fox allowing him to take such liberties without objection. To my amazement this little animal sat perfectly still while Ian, face close to the fox, had a good look right down to his eardrum! This fox was truly remarkable. The eardrum and canal proved of great interest to Ian, too. He pronounced it a fascinating and perfectly designed ear, slightly wider than that of a dog and with the actual drum slightly rounded.

I had to remind the vet that there might be some infection, so engrossed was he in what he was doing! He agreed that there was slight inflammation — and then said he wanted to have a look down the other ear! That, too, was absolutely fascinating (I remember distinctly that Ian was 'fascinated' because when I told Tom about it later on that day, his remark was 'Well, go on, tell me . . . how much did this FASCINATION cost us?') and he went on to say that it was the most perfect ear he had ever looked down. Ear drops, I was told, would have to be put in his ears three times a day for the next five days. I did not look forward to that task.

As Ian was so interested in the fox and his make-up I suggested he had a really good look at him while he was on the table; the fox, that is, not the vet. I showed him how dense and close the fur was, yet it was silky soft to the touch. He saw how the fur almost covered the pads on the feet. I ventured to suggest that this might give the fox a better grip in slippery conditions. He thought that quite likely.

Rachz allowed me to show his perfectly-formed,

sharp, white teeth. The canines were extremely long, slender and sharp. No doubt that they could rip flesh and kill with great ease.

Turning the fox on to his back I showed Ian how his fur covered his body totally. Unlike the dog, there was no sparse hair inside the thigh and on the belly. Instead, it was long and dense and thick, Nature's superb insulation against the most severe of elements.

Rachz accepted all this handling in a calm and relaxed manner. Naturally, I was talking to him all the time, telling him what a good boy he was, and so on, but even so, found it difficult to believe that he was so confident. Of course, the manner of the vet helped, too. Ian handled him gently and talked in a low voice.

Next it was the rabbit's turn. I held on to Rachz while Ian lifted the rabbit onto the table. I kept a good hold of the fox for obvious reasons, but even when the body of the rabbit inadvertently touched his flanks, he did not stir. Could it be that the fox was *so* frightened that this fear over-rode all other senses? If that was the case, why was he so calm. After all, he wasn't even trembling, nor was his heart beating any faster. And I am sure I would have *felt* his fear, if fear had been there at all. The rabbit did have 'snuffles' as I had thought and he was issued with antibiotic powder to go in his drinking water. It would not have been wise to take both animals out to the Landrover together, for fear of losing Rachz with only one hand free to hold him. So I asked Denise, the Head Nurse, if she would hold him while I put the rabbit in. She readily agreed to this and as she took Rachz I saw the look of panic in his eyes and he struggled as she held him. This time there was fear. But I knew Denise would cope with him for the few moments I was away. I have since thought about this and can only assume that since Rachz was away from his pen environment, then *I* was his refuge, so he had been quite happy for the vet to handle him as long as I was with him. Substitute Denise for myself, even for those few moments, and I took away from him all his feelings of security.

However, I soon had my fox back in my arms, into the Landrover and back home to his pen.

Whenever I go to the vet's I seem to get involved in talking to them and the nurses about all sorts of things, and end up forgetting to mention important things about my animals. This time I had forgotton to book a date for that all-important operation: castration.

Another telephone call and the date was fixed. Wednesday the 20th of October, 1982. There was just one more very important point to discuss and that was the question of stress. I asked if I could stay with Rachz until he was anæsthetized in order that the level of stress might be minimised. They were more than happy to oblige me in this request, for which they will always have my deepest gratitude. Prior to the day of the operation Rachz was to have no food after 6.00pm in order that his stomach might be empty, thus reducing the risk of vomiting whilst under the anæesthetic and food particles passing down his air passage.

October the 20th arrived. I packed Rachz into the back of the Landrover and must admit to wondering if I would see him alive again. Even though anæsthetics are extremely safe nowadays, there are always risks that something unforeseen could occur, such as, for instance, an epileptic fit. These thoughts troubled me all the way to the surgery, but I have total confidence in my vets and knew that if anything *did* go wrong they would be in no way to blame.

Rachz received star treatment within two minutes of arriving at the surgery. First of all he was given a sedative injection which rendered him sleepy within minutes. Then I carried him through to be weighed so that the correct dose of anæsthetic could be administered. From there we went into the consulting room where Ian plugged in the electric razor to remove the fur on Rachz's foreleg for the intravenous anæsthetic. It was here that we met with a slight problem. The fur was so dense that the razor was making absolutely no impression: another interesting feature about foxes. No wonder they can withstand the cold so well.

Another blade was used and this time, albeit still with some difficulty, the fur was shaved away. In went the injection which took effect immediately, and down his throat went the tube that was to be connected to the oxygen supply in the operating theatre. He was immediately whisked away by Ian and I went back to the waiting room.

It was no longer than fifteen or twenty minutes before Ian appeared and asked me into the consulting room again. There, laid out on the table, was my fox, operation over. He was still very much asleep, though, and Ian had other operations to get on with. So with instructions to me to keep his tongue hanging out of the side of his mouth, so that he did not choke, Ian said he would be back later to see how Rachz was. I talked to my fox and stroked him and was so pleased that all had gone well and that soon he would be home and safe.

Rachz took rather a long time coming round from the anæsthetic and I could tell that Ian was a little worried from the way he popped back in to see the fox every ten minutes. Eventually, the last operation was completed and Ian came in to try and get Rachz to respond by pinching his toes, flicking his ear and pulling on this foreleg.

The fox opened his eyes and then shut them again. By now I was a little concerned but Ian assured me that the fox was quite all right, just taking longer than expected to come round.

Another five or ten minutes passed and Ian decided that it would be all right to take Rachz out to the Landrover. I gently but firmly carried him out of the surgery, Ian going ahead of me to open the doors. We reached the Landrover, the door was opened and I went to lift the fox carefully into the back. Like greased lightning he was out of my arms and into the safety of the cardboard box!

Neither Ian nor I could believe this. All that time we had spent waiting for him to come round and he had been 'playing possum'! Before leaving I had further instructions not to feed him until late that day and then only to give him a small amount of food. Easier said than done!

I put Rachz into the kitchen when we arrived home and after having a bit of a nap he started wandering round the kitchen, then jumping up onto the workbench and from there to the windowsill. The food I had previously prepared for him was up there covered by a plate. Now that he had found his food there was no way he was going to come away from it!

I tried to pick him off the windowsill upon which he flattened his ears and growled and snarled, and wound himself round the dish so as to prevent me taking it from him. He was so obviously all right now that I relented, bearing in mind that it was thirtysix hours since he had eaten. Taking the plate off the food dish I left him up there to enjoy it. Which he did, and very quickly too. With a full tummy he was now a happy fox and any thoughts of being nasty had quite gone from his mind. I allowed him to stay in the house a little while longer, just to be quite sure he was not going to vomit and then, happy that it was all over, I took him out to his pen. The following morning he was back to his normal self, running about and jumping on and off the logs.

Animals are amazing. They go through the trauma of routine operations and twentyfour hours later it is as if they had had nothing done to them at all. All I had to do now was wait and see how quickly the castration operation worked on quietening him down.

Minced, cooked chicken goes down well!

Bob Hughes visits Rachz but ends up having his photo taken with Panda, Jai and Bajha.

CHAPTER TWELVE — *RACHZ CATCHES A HEN*

SHORTLY after Rachz had his operation Bob Hughes who, if you remember, was the man who rang me up wanting a home for the fox, contacted me asking if he and his family could come over to see how he was getting on. Naturally, I was delighted that he was still interested in Rachz and there and then a day and time were arranged. We all looked forward to this visit immensely and I was particularly keen to see if the fox remembered Bob and his family.

Everything was organised for the day they were to visit and I brought all the available chairs into the kitchen so that all concerned could have a ringside seat. I mentally played around with the best way to re-introduce the fox and finally decided that it would be best if he were in the kitchen to start with and the visitors would be brought in one by one so that he got used to the numbers slowly. I had also decided that it could help Rachz if Bajha were there, too, for added confidence, because with the dogs he showed no fear or apprehension at all.

The chocolate-drop container was filled to the brim, for I had no idea how many he would consume once we all got going with them.

Lunch that day was a quick and hurried affair and with plenty of time to spare we all sat waiting for Bob. The great moment had arrived as Bob and family drew up at the back door. Out here, in the country, everyone seems to use the back door — it virtually becomes the 'front door'. I ushered them all in via the conservatory, through the lounge and into the kitchen one by one, putting them into the seats that would provide the best view!

The whole episode was a total disaster. All the careful planning had come to nought. I was disappointed. Bob was disappointed. Everyone was really depressed. Rachz, the object of all this preparation, took one look at the first person entering the kitchen jumped up onto the top of one of the dog food bins situated under one of the workbenches and disappeared for the rest of the visit.

Kind words, Bob's special call for him, chocolate drops, Bajha, toys — nothing. No fox appeared and it soon became obvious that he had no intention of being seen at all. So much for the kindness Bob had shown him when he first took him from the man in the pub. I felt really sorry for Bob. He had travelled a long way from his home to come and see him. He must have felt so disappointed, though he kept on saying that it didn't matter. And so a forlorn group left the kitchen and went into the lounge for coffee where we were at least able to show the family the photographs we had taken of the fox. Bob and his family were very enamoured of the dogs and could not get over how good their temperaments were.

Aah! Perhaps this offered a chance of making the afternoon worthwhile. I suggested to Tom that it might be nice to take some photographs of the family with the dogs. Apparently, according to Bob, none of their friends would believe that they had all sat in a room with three German Shepherd Dogs. So a good few photographs were taken and I promised to send them a copy once we had them processed. I thought that since they were all here I might as well show them round and let them see all our other animals, and would include the pen Tom had built especially for Rachz. Thankfully, it was a very nice day and I hoped that showing them all the other animals would make up a little for the disappointment over Rachz.

The rest of the dogs were in the dog runs and they all leapt about in greeting as we passed. I have always prided myself on the exceptionally good temperaments I have managed to breed and knew that even though these particular dogs had not actually met Bob and his family they would react with nothing but friendliness if small fingers were poked through the mesh to stroke them. All our dogs adore meeting new people and I often say they are more like Golden Retrievers in temperament, than stand-offish German Shepherds.

First we came to the pen Tom had made for Rachz. Bob was quite impressed (just as well, for Tom had put a lot of work into it) but I got the feeling he thought it rather small. Eventually he said perhaps it would be a good idea to tether him outside for a while during the day. This may be a good idea in a back garden of a semi-detached house in the suburbs, but I thought it would be unwise to expect things to run as smoothly living out in the country, particularly bearing in mind that we had hens and ducks and geese — not to mention the cats! After a little more discussion I said that I would tether him while I was cleaning out his pen, which I did a couple of times a week. This meant I would be around to keep and eye on him in case of mishaps.

So we continued our walk around and showed them the birds and the pet rabbits. Every so often one of the cats would fly past obviously on the trail of something or the other. The cats did enjoy living here with all the undergrowth, bushes and fields to hunt mice and birds.

Sometimes I would find them asleep in a cosy place secluded but with the warmth of the sun streaming down and covering the cat with its glow. Soon it was time for Bob to make the journey back to Sunderland and as we waved 'Goodbye' to them I dearly wished the visit had been more successful.

A couple of days later it was time to clean the pen out, so I clipped the long lead onto Rachz and having brought him out then tied the other end to the outside of the dogs run, about ten feet from where I would be working. He took to this very well and spent a lot of time sniffing around and trying to dig holes. Satisfied that he would keep himself amused while I did the necessary chores, I quickly checked around to make sure that there were no hens or ducks lurking in a dangerous position and started clearing out the straw and sweeping the pen out. All of a sudden there was a squawk and rustle of wings and I whipped round. To my horror Rachz had hold of one of the hens by its throat! The bird must have wandered through and being quite used to the dogs walked within easy pouncing distance — and the fox had acted instinctively with the skill and timing that thousands of years had imprinted in his mind. Living in captivity had not dulled the instinct for survival, even though the need for food had never made it necessary for the fox to draw upon this inherited reaction.

If Rachz had acted instinctively, then now I did. Using the commanding voice that I keep for the dogs when they are doing something they shouldn't I uttered five words. 'Rachz — leave it! Leave it!'

I don't know what I was expecting him to do. As I have just said, I spoke instinctively. All I can say is that the hours of talking to the fox, petting him and socialising

Aleta is not too sure . . . . .

. . . . . but Nancy takes meeting a fox in her stride.

him, must have come to mean something to him, for he did
the last thing I would have expected him to do. HE LET
THE HEN GO!

To my further astonishment the hen appeared
unharmed, for it staggered away, looking a little shocked
(it was probably VERY shocked) but nonetheless still on
its feet.

Rachz at this point, though still in a very good position
to attack the hen again, simply lay back on his haunches
with his ears flat against the side of his head and an
expression of guilt written all over his face. I can only
assume that he had picked up my tone of displeasure from
when he played too roughly with the dogs and I would tell
him off for pulling their tail too hard or biting an ear and
hanging on.

Even the cats if I see them with a bird or a mouse, do
not let their prey go when I shout at them — they just
glower menacingly at me, daring me to take the matter
any further, and then take to their heels, disappearing into
dense undergrowth where they can finish what they
started. That this fox should have reacted in the way he
did I shall always marvel at.

We did go after the hen to see if it *was* all right, but
Rachz had just about torn its throat open and it had to be
put to sleep. So it joined the other deceased pets in our
little graveyard.

Each time I recounted this tale to friends they asked
me how I felt towards the fox now that this had happened.
I had to tell them, quite truthfully, that I felt no animosity
towards him at all. It was all very unfortunate but only
one person could be held responsible and that was me.
How could I hold it against the fox for reacting the way he
did? One thing was for sure. There would be no more

tethering in the field or anywhere else. He would get his exercise in future as he had it in the past and that would eliminate any risk to the other livestock.

There was now another job to be done for Rachz in order that he might be made more comfortable. He needed larger premises which would give him space to move now that he had grown and where he would be able to see the sky and trees above him.

*The isolation kennel that Tom built is turned into
a new home for Rachz.*

Rachz peers through his 'pop-hole'.

CHAPTER THIRTEEN — *LARGER PREMISES*

THE PEN that Tom had built for Rachz was a work of art, but now that the fox was outgrowing it and becoming bored living in it, the obvious step was to convert other animals' premises or build him a new one.

With the number of animals we had to look after and feed money was always a bit tight and it was soon patently obvious that we could not afford to build the fox another, larger pen. In the 'bottom field' we had already erected a large shed and Tom had built a very nice slab-wood fence round it. This was to be our 'isolation kennel' for bitches when they came into season. It had, in fact, been used for that purpose, very successfully, ever since it was finished. But now it was to be converted especially for Rachz.

Foxes dig, everyone told me, over and over again. I had been told so many times that it had become an obsession with me and since the base of the 'run' was still only hardpacked soil I had to think hard about how I was going to stop Rachz digging his way out.

First, though, I decided to line the shed with some of the pallets mentioned previously. In doing this I would eliminate the possibility of him chewing through the single layer of wood and escaping. To this end I sawed and hammered, hammered and sawed, working all the spare hours I could find. Most pieces I managed to cut to the correct size, others were too big or too small. In the end, after about a week, it was finished. I was really pleased with the little den I had made him inside the shed, with a 'pop-hole' and removable lid! This I then filled with fresh, crunchy, yellow straw; and put plenty of sawdust onto the floor.

The next job in this marathon task I had set myself was to line the inside of the pen with pallets, too. Compared to the shed this was a simple and fairly quick job and I merrily hammered my way through the following three or four days until that was complete.

The penultimate job was to require my heartiest efforts: making a hard base to the run. It would be no good whatsoever using little bricks and stones to do this so the only material suitable was the enormous stones that lay in heaps around our land. In their heyday they had stood proudly in the form of dry-stone walls. Now, with the advent of posts and wire they had been pushed aside, becoming almost covered from view by long straggly grass and harbouring spiders and woodlice, grubs and worms. These, then, were to become the base of the pen and just how all those dry-stone walls were made to meander over hills and dales in northern England I do not know. Have you ever picked up any of the larger ones? They are back-breaking!

The wheelbarrow came in useful. I stacked it high with enormous blocks of stone only to find that once loaded it was impossible to move it anywhere! So eventually I became expert on how many and of what shape and size to put in the barrow so that I could then move them to the pen. It took me three days to move the required amount from various and sometimes almost inaccessible parts of the land. Often the only time I had available was in the evenings and sometimes as the moon rose it would look down to see Philippa holding a torch for me while I trundled back and forth collecting boulders.

On the fourth day I started laying the boulders — it is useless calling them stones — and I ached all over from the effort of lifting weights upwards of 60 lbs and carrying them into the pen to be laid. Laying them required further effort and concentration as I endeavoured to fit them like pieces of a jig-saw with the minimum number of gaps between them. Mostly a reasonable level was maintained, but since the boulders varied considerably in depth it was impossible to get the surface perfectly flat. When it was all done the effect was one of a natural terrain. To finish it off I purloined some of Tom's gravel and filled all the gaps and hollows. It looked very nice, but, boy, was I pleased to see the end of it!

So that Rachz could not slip out between my legs when I went into the pen I sank two posts into the ground in front of, and close to, the gate posts and nailed some boarding across the front. This way, when I opened the gate inwards, I then stepped over the three foot barrier, into the pen and shut the gate behind me with the aid of a bolt.

The final job was left for Tom and that was to stretch some strong wire over the top of the pen and down the back where the slab-wood was rather thin.

Now that the shed and pen were strong and secure against escape I could dwell on what to put inside to give the fox exercise. A large tree had fallen during a storm one night and had since been cut into even lengths. I pushed and pulled two of these into the pen and stood them on end, making sure they were very secure among the boulders. Planks of wood were then nailed along the top making a running ledge where Rachz could jump on and off and which would enable him to watch what was going on outside, since the pen itself was solid up to half the height. A drinking bowl for his water, some toys, a few small logs of wood for him to chew on, a larger bowl for him to paddle in if he wanted to, a pop-hole in the shed door, chain and THREE locks on the pen door and it was all ready for him.

The following morning all the family were up early to see Rachz in his new quarters. Lifting him out of his old pen for the last time I carried him gently the fifty yards to his new home. Once inside and the gate locked we all peered in to see what he would do.

With extreme caution he crept about examining everything he came into contact with. As the moments passed and he acclimatised himself to his new surroundings he visibly relaxed and was soon running about, tail held high and with sheer pleasure showing in his eyes.

We tried, by calling him, to encourage him up onto one of the ledges, to no avail. So I placed a few chocolate drops through the wire on to one of them and knew that eventually he would scent them and would have to jump up to get them. I was not to know then that putting him into this new place where there was so much more room and where I could go in with him, was to be yet another turning point in socialising him. He was, by this time, about seven months old.

It was lovely to be able to go in and have him pulling at my jeans in play, running around and hiding behind the logs, with just his little face showing with those beautiful amber eyes full of trust and intelligence.

By this time he had almost grown his full coat and his tail, or should I call it 'brush'. He was a beautiful fox in superb condition, each hair lying straight and glistening

Caught in the act of digging a hole to bury some food.

Rachz hides behind a large tree trunk.

in the sun. His legs were a deep bitter-chocolate brown and so were the backs of his ears, which now looked better proportioned. The muzzle was long and strong and the lips were free of any looseness. The nails on his toes were dark and firm and now that he was on hard ground I knew they would be worn down naturally — whoever heard of a fox having its nails clipped?!

But I digress. Before I tell you how his temperament and character progressed I have to let you know of a new worry that beset me.

The worry I had was for the fox's safety. For the pen was situated much further from the house than his original one and at night that portion of the field was pitch black. We had had poachers in the vicinity in the past and this was my worry now. But how was I to protect Rachz?

At night, in bed, with the window wide open, my ears took in every sound that drifted towards me on the night air. If a duck quacked or one of the dogs shifted in the kennel I was up, peering through the blackness towards the pen, trying to pick out any movement that meant trouble for the fox. Seeing nothing, I would go back to bed, but not to sleep. I listened, still, for everything and heard sounds that would not normally bother me. A dog barking maybe two miles away, voices carried across the fields, a cow mooing three fields away, the crack of a branch as it hit another one with the wind. When it was windy I was worse, for the wind muffled any slight sounds.

I did not sleep for three nights, so afraid was I that if I did, someone would come and take my fox away. Obviously I had to do something about this fear of a real or imagined danger if I was not to become nocturnal like a fox — though if *I* did not sleep at night there was certainly no way I could sleep during the day either! While I was wondering what to do about it permanently I had the bright idea of leaving two of the dogs out in their runs during the night. That way they would see and hear anything suspicious and their barking would awaken me. Hopefully I could at last get some sleep.

So for the next two nights Bajha and Sherpa watched in amazement while I carried their kennel carpets into the runs and told them to go to bed on them. They were flabbergasted. They could not believe that I meant it. I was not worried about them — the weather was good and the night air though fresh, was not cold.

When I looked out of the bedroom window I could see them and both were settled on their beds, heads on paws, but alert. As neither of them barked just for the sake of it I knew I would not be woken unnecessarily — only if someone was on the land.

There was a shed that we used to put the geese in at night which had blown over during a particularly bad storm — fortunately the birds were not in at the time — and since it was in the vicinity of the fox's pen it seemed a good idea to move it to the other end of the run, anchor it by sinking posts in the ground and putting a couple of the dogs to bed in it at night.

This job was done as quickly as possible. Two dogs were put in at night, or if I had to go out during the day. I hasten to add that this was quite a large shed and both dogs were very comfortable in it. Then, as an added precaution, another of the dogs was left in the field itself, free to roam around at night, but unable to get through any of the fencing that surrounded our fields. At last Rachz had all the protection that he deserved. Frequently during the day I would walk up and see him and on calling his name he would squeak and wag his tail furiously. At

What's that! Rachz sees something of interest outside his pen.

Stop taking my photograph – I'm trying to get some sleep!

times the tail would cause the fox some concern, for I do not suppose foxes wag their tails much in the wild. The pleasure of seeing me, or one of the dogs, would get this tail wagging to such an extent that Rachz would turn round to see what it was doing, as if it shouldn't really be doing it at all. Anyone who thinks that foxes do not wag their tail with pleasure, like a dog does, is quite wrong. Maybe other foxes have not wagged their tales — but this one most definitely DOES. There is no doubt about that. I tried to keep Rachz happily occupied by giving him 'toys' such as rinsed-out washing up liquid bottles, the cardboard rolls inside kitchen foil, small cardboard boxes and the like.

Large clumps of grass made their appearance in the field and I would dig up two or three of these so that Rachz could play with them and toss them about and tear at them. Occasionally I would arrive at the pen to find him 'digging' in the large water bowl, in play, sometimes having previously dropped one of his toys in. So on the whole I kept him interested and happy.

He still went out into the field on his long lead for exercise and digging holes, but now I only felt it necessary to do this twice a week. It was usually later on in the day that I did this as he spent most of the afternoons asleep in his den or on one of the ledges I had put up for him.

Whenever he saw one of the dogs in the 'run' he became very excited and did his usual squeaking and wagging of the tail act, pulling me over to the wire so that he could sniff noses with them.

By this time Bajha had become bored with playing with the fox and if I took him out into the field he would play for a while before his male instinct took him off to have a scout around.

Bahli was one of the bitches that I thought too flighty for Rachz to meet before, but she was older now and had settled down a bit. One day before I got the fox out into the field for his run I put Bahli in the field. As soon as Rachz has his lead on and saw the dog he jumped out of his pen and rushed up to her. She was a little dubious at first, not having met him before, but soon regained her confidence and they started playing.

The fox decided to run — so the dog ran after him. Rachz had played like this with Bajha before and as he ran he egged the dog on, by suddenly turning and nipping at her legs as he passed.

Very soon they were both exhausted. Never before had the fox had such a good time. He had literally jumped over Bahli a few times and rolled on his back for her to come up to him and nuzzle his belly, upon which he would grab a leg and roll about underneath her. Then there would be another running session where he would twist and turn with great agility, then rush away to dig a hole. Bahli would join him and they would both look up with soil all over their faces!

So Bahli became his 'play companion' since she, unlike Bajha was not interested in anything but playing with the fox. I was so pleased, for although foxes are on the whole, lone animals, Rachz obviously enjoyed company on occasions and she fitted the bill superbly. Other times I would go into his pen and play with him in there, perhaps taking with me an old pair of socks, so that he could play tug-of-war with them and me. It was at times like this that I noticed another trait. Anything new, and he would rub his gums along it. Two or three times. I could only think that this must be some form of scent transference from him to the object, or possibly a method of 'tasting' the scent of

What a fat fox! Rachz accepts a chocolate drop from Philippa

*Rachz watches with a worried expression
while his run is hosed down.*

the strange article. I don't know, but he did it on many occasions — even with the small logs of wood that I put in for him to chew at.

Rachz always knew when I had chocolate drops about my person and he would push his sharp little nose into the pocket, scratching away with his forefeet at the same time until either he managed to reach them himself or I got some out for him.

I taught him to come when he was called both in the field, when he was on his lead, and in the pen by singing out 'Ra-a-a-chz, come and see, come and see.' When he came he received a chocolate drop and very soon he was 'coming' every time. I continued with the 'sit' as well and he learnt to do that for a titbit, too. BUT, I never called him to me if, for instance I had to put drops in his ears. Under those sort of circumstances I always went to HIM. I did not want him to be suspicious about coming to me when I called him.

Although the fox liked playing in his water bowl he did not like the hose-pipe when I took it up the field to scrub down his pen and run, which I did once a week. Those times he would 'take to his bed' and only peer out occasionally just to keep an eye on things.

He found a few places in the run where he could dig. Little nooks and crannies where the stones did not fit perfectly. Mounds of soil and gravel would appear overnight, but I was not worried about this since the hole was very small and it gave him something to do. There were other times, however, when he dug holes to bury morsels of food that he did not want to eat at that moment. Lumps of cheese, bits of meat, eggs and dog biscuits all went into little holes that were then neatly covered by Rachz using his nose to move the soil back into place.

Instinct taking over again, you see.

Regarding his food. For a long time he would panic if anyone went near him while he was eating, and he would grab a mouthful and run away, growling, ears pressed flat against his head and eyes narrowed. But as time went by he became much more confident and would allow me to stroke him while he was eating, and eventually he would actually approach me as I arrived with dish in hand, and climb up my legs to see what there was for supper, grabbing bits out of the dish if there was anything particularly tasty.

So the summer months passed — I would often just sit in the pen with him, talking to him and stroking him. Or take him out in the field and sit on the grass while he sniffed around and dug a hole or two. Naturally, I am hoping to have this fox his entire natural life but I wanted to touch him and feel his soft fur, so that when I no longer had him I could still remember the feel of him and see his wonderful eyes. Whenever I did go into the run I would always have chocolate drops with me and spend a lot of time encouraging Rachz to approach me. While he was eating the treat and was within reaching distance, I would stretch out my hand and scratch his chest, gradually moving my hand so that I would be tickling under his arms and work my way round to his rib-cage.

It was a while before he was totally relaxed at me taking these liberties, but I would always talk to him in a soft voice. When a few weeks of this had passed I was able to run my hand over his head and onto his back, digging my finger deep into his fur and scratching hard. He really liked this and would crane his neck forward and shut his eyes with the pleasure of it. He would stay like this for a couple of minutes and then, that was it, he had had

Mission accomplished!

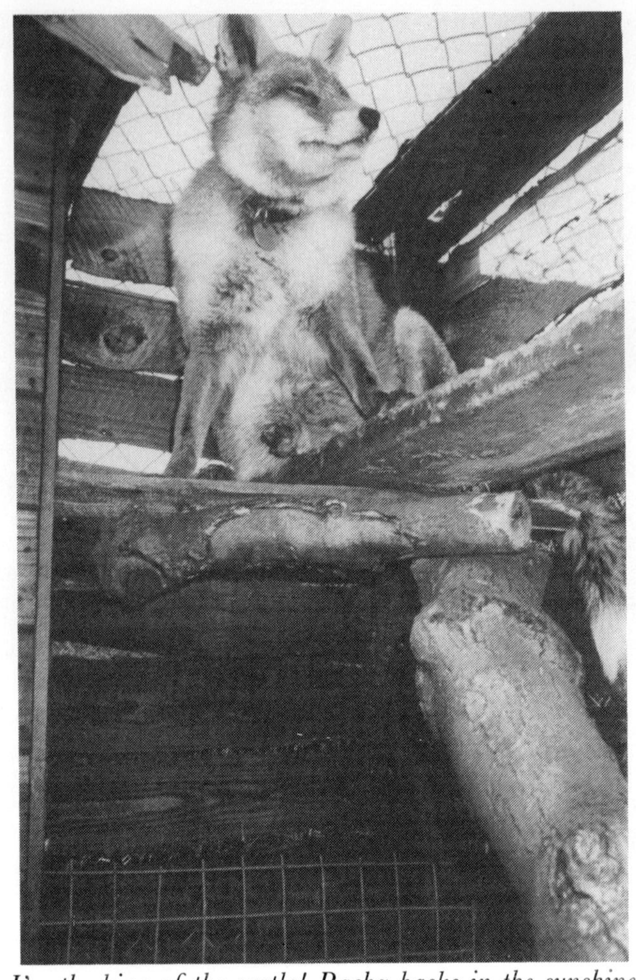

I'm the king of the castle! Rachz basks in the sunshine.

enough and would suddenly turn and grab my hand for a play! Soon he and I were sniffing noses, though I could tell he was a bit overawed at his own braveness when he did this. One day I put a chocolate drop between my lips and offered it to him. Initially his approach was by stretching his neck forward but keeping the rest of his body as far away as possible. Once he got used to treats offered in this way he became very adept at taking them.

It was interesting the way he did this, too, for there was no sudden snatch. Just a gentle muzzle, lips drawn back so as not to be in the way, reaching out, ever so gently, ever so softly and taking it from me with his front teeth. When you think back to the incident of the hen that he attacked I find it remarkable that his contact with another kind of flesh was so different.

I was never worried that he might suddenly snap or bite — it is just not in him to do that to me. An action such as he was doing, coming into such close contact with a human being, must surely dispel any thoughts that foxes are sly and unreliable. In the wild, possibly, for they have to rely on their wits to survive. But a fox tamed and loved and given confidence is a wonderful thing to have known.

I have been unable, so far, to take a photograph of him taking a treat from my lips since he is a little camera-shy if someone else is taking them. One day perhaps.

Suddenly, as always seems to happen without warning, the days became shorter, chill winds began to sweep the air and leaves shrivelled and floated to the ground. Autumn was upon us and I often watched Rachz when there was windy weather, for he would stand, head lifted, nostrils taking in each and every scent borne his way, eyes almost closed. What messages the wind brought him I shall never know, for I had no way of finding out.

We still had the runs in the field, sometimes in the pouring rain for I gave no thought to my own comfort where this animal was concerned.

The rain mangified the earthbound scents and the fox and I would wander round the hedgerows while he sniffed around and I got wet! What did it matter? Who was I to complain about getting wet when it was my privilege to be exercising this fox. He was doing me the favour of being with me, not the other way round. He was looking robust and healthy and his coat was so very thick and dense, in readiness for the scourges of winter. The fur on the main part of his body was rich red-gold, while that of his underbelly and inner thighs was grey interspersed with white. The top of his brush was a brilliant white, just as if it had been dipped into household gloss paint! Yes, he was certainly ready for winter.

CHAPTER FOURTEEN — *WINTER*

RAGING WINDS and torrential rain preceded the first fall of snow. When it came, it came silently and unseen by most. Quietly through the sky the flakes fell, twirling and lifting before finally coming to rest on the cold, hard ground. Flake fell upon flake until finally the sheer weight moulded them all together and their individual, intricate pattern disappeared for all time. As we crawled out from under our blankets to the call of another day the world, or so it seemed, jealous of us warm and comfortable in our beds, had produced its own blanket.

Shimmering, soft, glistening, clinging — what words can describe that wonder that is snow? God must surely have created snow to bring to the drabness of winter a touch of magic, for does not snow make one gasp at first sight at the sheer beauty of it?

I was anxious to see how Rachz had fared during the night and hurriedly dressed and ran down to his pen. He was sitting on one of the ledges, looking around him with interest. The wire mesh covering the top of his pen had captured every flake that fell its way and it had been transformed into a beautiful piece of lace. I touched the wire, causing a few dustings of snow to fall. Rachz watched this, tongue out, eyes alight. He jumped off the ledge, landing softly in the deep snow. Pushing his nose into its interesting depths he breathed deeply, then emerged with a blob of snow on the end of his nose! I love watching animals when they first see snow. Cats are the funniest as they try very hard to gauge their path so that they only walk where it is shallow: usually an impossible task as they find themselves sinking up to their armpits with each step and the further away they go the further they have to come back! This fox, however, was obviously going to enjoy every minute of it.

Imagine how surprised he was going to be after burying food in the snow to wake up one day after the snow had melted to find it all sitting on top of the stones!

The bottom field dips along one side so there would be a good three to four foot drift along there and I was looking forward to seeing how Rachz reacted in snow that deep. Forcing the snow back into the pen as I opened the door I climbed in and soon had the fox on his lead. Once out in the field he sniffed and dived in the snow, running this way and that. He would stop occasionally to dig a hole, then, having investigated what was at the bottom of it, would carry on until he decided it was time to dig another one. Eventually we came to the side of the field where the deep drift was and I started running alongside it. He followed me, jumping and twisting and turning and diving headlong into the drift he disappeared except for his tail. He loved it. And I loved seeing him enjoy it so much. We both ran up and down this side of the field until we were exhausted.

As soon as the fox was covered in snow all he had to do was shake himself and every single bit came off him. That coat he had grown for the winter was certainly paying dividends now. Nature's superb insulation! Though I suppose a fox in the wild, even though it may have a good coat for the elements, would be affected if it had not had sufficient food to build up its reserves in other ways.

Rachz stayed snug and dry in his shed, coming out into the fields to play in the snow or, in his pen, he would spend his time digging holes or simply lying on one of the ledges soaking up what warmth the sun threw his way. As winter receded and the first glimmerings of Spring became apparent Rachz was fast nearing the end of his first year.

CHAPTER FIFTEEN — *ONE YEAR OLD*

MARCH AND Rachz was now one year old and I had been fortunate to watch him change and grow and develop from the age of about ten weeks. I had found out his likes and dislikes in the way of food and helped him grow into a fine adult fox. Possibly there would always be a lack of maturity about him, with having him castrated, but that would be all.

Time had been spent with him to help him grow to trust me and I had played with him and brought forth dog-like qualities that maybe few people would have the pleasure of experiencing. In particular the incident where he picked out my scent on twigs will always stay with me. Everything about that fox will always stay with me even when he is no more.

Many people chance upon an opportunity of a lifetime. It may be breeding the finest pigeon or climbing the highest tree or mountain. For me it has been owning Rachz. Such a beautfiful creature and I have been able to observe him at close quarters. Even so, having the fox brings me sadness, too. For he should really be free. Free to run as many miles as he wishes and to mate and reproduce his kind; living his life through the seasons and being part of them. I have done, and will continue to do, the very best I can by him but one thing is certain. I will never keep another fox captive again. Their rightful place is where their will takes them, unhindered. To watch the sun rise from a leafy bed under a fallen tree and to stalk through the woods experiencing all that they hold. One day he will run free but that will be when his spirit departs this life. I hope there is a heaven for animals, for if I am lucky enough to chance upon the same path I will be re-united with my lovely Rachz once more.